kamer

BOOKS

CW00456572

kamerabooks.com

I AM NOT A NUMBER

DECODING *THE PRISONER*

ALEX COX

kamera
BOOKS

First published in 2017 by Kamera Books,
an imprint of Oldcastle Books,
PO Box 394, Harpenden, Herts, AL5 1XJ
www.kamerabooks.com

A CIP catalogue record for this book is available from the British Library.

ISBN
978-0-85730-175-8 (print)
978-0-85730-177-2 (epub)
978-0-85730-178-9 (kindle)
978-0-85730-179-6 (pdf)

2 4 6 8 10 9 7 5 3

Design and typeset by Elsa Mathern
Printed and bound by CPI Group (UK) Ltd, Croydon, CR0 4YY

FOR PABLO

CONTENTS

INTRODUCTION

When *The Prisoner* was first broadcast in 1967 and 1968 I thought it was the best thing I had ever seen on TV. I was barely a teenager, watched quite a lot of telly, and had never seen the like. Fifty years later, having re-watched all the episodes, repeatedly, I feel exactly the same way. We're often told today that episodic television has replaced the cinema as 'intellectual' narrative fare. I don't think this is true. While mainstream cinema has never been less intellectually challenging, modern episodic TV is in its own unique ways equally dull. More happens in two hours of *McCabe & Mrs. Miller* than in an entire season of *Deadwood*. Contemporary episodic TV takes one idea and runs very slowly with it. Supporting characters who would be given one line of dialogue in a feature film have whole episodes and subplots devoted to them. And series never end - instead each season 'concludes' with a bunch of cliffhangers and unresolved characters - because the goal is to rack up the episodes. TV is bought and sold in bulk, and 100 episodes is the goal.

The Prisoner could not have been more different. The first season had thirteen episodes, each discrete unto itself. Every episode was intellectually challenging, disturbing, and remarkably prescient. The hero and a couple of apparent villains were the only recurring characters. The early, standalone, episodes presented dire threats to The Prisoner. In how many other shows was the protagonist threatened with a 'leucotomy'? Who even knew what a 'leucotomy' was? But, as the series proceeded, the threats receded, and *The Prisoner* was able to game The Village and influence events there. Blows were frequently exchanged, but until the final episodes guns were never seen. An aura of enforced politeness and cleanliness of body and mind prevailed. There seemed no escape from the pretty seaside resort town known as The Village – but who ran it? Who was The Prisoner? What information did he have? Who were his captors, and why were they so desperate to break him? And who was Number 1?

In this book, I'll try to answer these questions. I believe that there are answers to be found, that they are contained in the 17 episodes of *The Prisoner*, in its scripts, in its story notes, and nowhere else. So, I'm not going to consider *Danger Man*, the TV series which made Patrick McGoohan a star, nor his subsequent work as an actor, nor – for the most part – the enigmatic and elusive interviews he gave regarding the series. McGoohan remarked that everything one needed to know was contained within those 17 episodes: asking for additional information would have meant that the series had failed. His point is an excellent one. McGoohan's series is free-standing, concrete, intelligent, and can be interpreted on its own terms, on the basis of what it contains.

The Prisoner is a complex whole, rooted in the Cold War, but even more deeply embedded in its Britishness (I almost wrote Englishness, since the series is so London-centric, but that would not do when its most memorable location was Portmeirion, in Wales). McGoohan, born in New York, could be American, English, or Irish as it suited him. But the clipped, public-school tones of Number 6 are the hallmark of a certain type of Englishman, and it is that character, and his relationship with his world, which I will explore here.

The Cold War was characterised by spying, surveillance, propaganda, and the amassing of vast nuclear arsenals. All are featured here. In the 1960s, Britain was in the process of giving up what remained of her Empire, and becoming increasingly dependent, militarily and economically, on the United States. While refusing to commit troops in Vietnam, Britain remained a dedicated member of NATO, the Americans' nuclear-armed alliance against Russia – the other big player in the Cold War. In the west, Russia was always our perceived antagonist, together with its Eastern European satellites, and the Asian communist countries, principally China. Russia and China actually had very little in common and disagreed on most issues, but in the minds of American war-planners and fiction writers the 'Iron Curtain' countries were all the same, both octopus and monolith. So, when the Chinese brainwash American GIs in *The Manchurian Candidate*, there are Russian advisors present. And when the North Vietnamese keep American GIs prisoner in *Rambo*, there are Russian advisors lurking behind the tiger cages.

Numerous were the sixties TV shows in which valiant British and American secret agents outsmarted and outgunned their

Russian counterparts. Few indeed were shows which suggested that the two sides might be fundamentally alike, and neither worth fighting for. Indeed, there was only one series which raised that issue: *The Prisoner*. But the series went far beyond secret agent craft, frequently dealing with the perversion of medical science for military and intelligence purposes. It dealt with the state of the art – as it then was – of Mind Control, something which obsessed both CIA and KGB; as we shall see, *The Prisoner* was both knowledgeable and prescient about this hideous quasi-science.

Patrick McGoohan had been the star of the popular British TV series, *Danger Man*, which was picked up by the American networks – something all British producers dreamed of. At the end of the third season of *Secret Agent* (as the Americans knew it), McGoohan approached the TV mogul Lew Grade, and proposed they make a different series together. Grade wanted another season of *Danger Man* – more than one, ideally – but he also wanted to keep McGoohan on board. He didn't read treatments or scripts, so, at a six am meeting, McGoohan made him a verbal pitch for the new show.

McGoohan showed Grade photographs of Portmeirion, where several episodes of *Danger Man* had been filmed. In this picturesque, Italianate Welsh village, he said, he wanted to shoot a series called *The Prisoner*. We don't know how exactly McGoohan pitched the show, nor whether he mentioned his collaborator, George Markstein – *Danger Man*'s most recent story editor. Markstein had told McGoohan of a secret government 'holiday camp' in Scotland – run by an entity called the Inter-Services Research Bureau – where defunct or dubious intelligence agents were detained, in comfort, during the Second World War. When he gave interviews in later years, Markstein insisted that The Prisoner was John

Drake, McGoohan's character from *Danger Man*. According to Markstein, Drake, a spy in the James Bond mould, quit the British secret service and was kidnapped – by one side or the other – so that he could be thoroughly debriefed in an ISRB-type camp. It's possible McGoohan gave Lew Grade the idea that these were Drake's further adventures – but in later years he would insist that The Prisoner was not Drake, and that his take on the project was not Markstein's.

Whatever the pitch contained, it worked. Grade's company, ITC, would fund a series called *The Prisoner*, starring McGoohan. It would be produced by McGoohan's company, Everyman Films, and McGoohan would act as executive producer. Presumably, if the series was successful, ITC would finance a second season. Each episode was given a budget of around £75,000. McGoohan, earning £2,000 a week, was said to be Britain's highest-paid actor. No doubt reassuring to Grade and ITC, the series would involve a number of key crew from *Danger Man*: David Tomblin, who had been an AD and 2nd unit director on *Danger Man*, would be the producer; George Markstein would be the script editor; Brendan Stafford, chosen as DP, had shot all the *Danger Man* episodes; Jack Shampan, having left *Danger Man* to work as art director on *Modesty Blaise*, rejoined McGoohan for *The Prisoner*; Frank Maher was fight arranger (and double for McGoohan) on both series; Rose Tobias-Shaw, the casting director, goes unmentioned in *Prisoner* literature, yet her contribution to both series was crucial – she cast 86 episodes of *Danger Man*, and all *The Prisoner* episodes. After *The Prisoner* she embarked on a feature film career which included *The Seven-Per-Cent Solution* and *Equus*.

On 3 September 1966, the London-based cast and crew boarded a train at Paddington station. Their destination was Portmeirion, nine hours away, where all the exteriors of the early episodes were to be filmed. The shoot began on Monday 5 September. Production was logistically complicated as only partial episodes could be shot at Portmeirion. Interiors would be filmed on sets yet to be built at MGM Studios, outside London. One set was The Prisoner's cottage interior; another was a vast circular space which served as Number 2's office, the Control Room, the Town Hall council chamber, and other locations. Scenes here often involved rear-projections of Portmeirion exteriors or of The Prisoner's cottage set; technical considerations like these (and the use of matte shots) dictated the order in which scenes were shot, and meant that no episode would be finished for several months. There were two principal Portmeirion shoots: the first one, involving McGoohan, and a second-unit shoot later in the season, when Frank Maher was used. McGoohan revisited Portmeirion with a mini-unit on subsequent weekends. Other exteriors were shot at the studio outside London, or in the city itself.

The first episode, *Arrival*, aired in Britain on 29 September 1967 – more than a year later. The first season was still in production. Was the public reaction to the first episodes bad? Had something changed in the relationship of McGoohan and Grade? Even before the first season, thirteen episodes long, was finished, word came down that ITC would not complete the second season – instead, there would be only four more episodes.

Or did it? This has been the 'official' version of this tale for many years. But the *Unmutual* website has unearthed a CBS press release, reported in the *Kansas City Star* dated 23 October 1966, about their acquisition of *The Prisoner, a 17-part series*, from ITC. Was this a typo? Was there a seventeen-episode *minimum guarantee* by ITC? Steven Davies has pointed out that while a 'prime time' US season was 13 weeks, a less-prestigious summer season might run to more episodes. Did CBS distrust the series, even while buying it, and hedge their bets by requesting extra episodes? In a script meeting for *Living in Harmony*, McGoohan told the screenwriter, Ian Rakoff, that he didn't know how many *Prisoner* episodes there would ultimately be: it could be 13, 17, or 26. Later, he said he felt seven was the ideal number. Everyman Films had commissioned at least two additional scripts, *Don't Get Yourself Killed*, by Gerald Kelsey, and *The Outsider*, by Moris Farhi, and had prepared synopses for further episodes. Frank Maher, McGoohan's double, called the 17 cut-off a complete surprise: he and the rest of the crew had been booked, they thought, for 26 shows.

The first, 13-part, season of *The Prisoner* was shot by the end of October 1967. Production on the last four episodes began the following month. The short second season was all filmed (though not edited) before the end of the year. The best source for when episodes were shot is always the production call sheet. These are more reliable than production schedules, which encompass an entire picture or series and are subject to change. Call sheets are written and distributed the night before the shoot, and – unless there was an unexpected incident or accident – can be relied upon as accurate. (Another reliable resource would be camera reports with scene numbers, but I haven't seen any of these. Fortunately, some call sheets, together with the series' scripts, were made available as 'extras' on DVD and Blu-ray sets.)

Legend has it that McGoohan wrote the last episode, *Fall Out*, in 36 hours, and that it was broadcast on British TV only two weeks later. It's certainly possible the prolific writer/director/producer/actor wrote the screenplay in a fast, creative frenzy; but the shoot itself wasn't a quick one. Making *The Prisoner* was a difficult logistical process, and the notion that the last, and most complex, episode could be shot, edited, and delivered in two weeks is an unlikely one. Fortunately, we have the call sheets for *Fall Out*. These show twelve days of shooting during the month of November 1967, together with scenes from another episode, *The Girl Who Was Death*. *Fall Out* was in the can before December 1967 and was broadcast on 1 February 1968. So, there were two months, not two weeks, to get the editing done.

The Prisoner is an extraordinary piece of work: a continuous planning/production/editing process which stretched for almost a year and a half, and produced seventeen remarkable films. It was the product of a big team, an excellent and ever-changing cast, and a dedicated creative core: McGoohan, Markstein, Tomblin, Shampan, and Tobias-Shaw. Markstein was crucial to the early episodes, selecting the writers and giving them the 'pitch'; increasingly at odds with McGoohan, he quit after the first season. In Markstein's absence, Tomblin became more important, writing and directing his own episodes. At the outset, McGoohan was intensely involved with almost all production aspects. He wrote and directed, and fired two or three directors on set, taking over their duties. Yet towards the end of the first season, his commitment waned. He was absent for some time, acting in a Hollywood action movie. So one episode – ironically, one of the best – features another actor playing his character. It's been suggested that McGoohan took the Hollywood job so as to be able to fund the last four episodes. This seems unlikely. ITC owned the series, and was paying for it. Everyman, the production company owned by McGoohan and Tomblin, was making *The Prisoner*, but wasn't the financier.

The chapters which follow will deal with each of the episodes. Every episode but one provides the viewer with consistent information – about The Village, about The Prisoner, about his captors and their relationship with London and the Cold War –

all of which adds up, I believe, to a complicated but consistent vision, and in the aggregate provides an answer to its persistent questions: who is The Prisoner? Why did he resign? Who or what is Number 1? The wild-card episode is *Do Not Forsake Me Oh My Darling*, made in McGoohan's absence, which fundamentally contradicts the other episodes, as we shall see.

'Questions are a burden to others; answers a prison for oneself'. Signs in the Labour Exchange tell us this in the first episode of *The Prisoner*. Nevertheless, in the *Decoding* chapter I'll try to provide unambiguous answers to the puzzles this extraordinary work of art contains.

Any complex work is open to multiple interpretations: *Moby Dick* would not be a great novel, nor *The Prisoner* a great dramatic series, if they didn't inspire confusion, argument, and impassioned disagreements among their fierce adherents. But we don't look for the meaning of *Moby Dick* by reading *White Jacket*, or an evasive interview Herman Melville gave to *Spin* magazine. *The meaning of the piece is contained within the text, and only there.*

For that reason, in the following chapters I'm going to consider the episodes in the order in which they were made. I know this is contrary to the way they're normally viewed, which tends to follow the British broadcast sequence. But *The Prisoner* was a creative project which developed as it went along. Of course, much was known about it at the outset – especially by McGoohan. Markstein created a four-page 'bible' titled *T.V. Series – Working Title – The Prisoner*, which sets a template for the conflict and the environment of the whole series. But much more came to be known as the story developed, episode by episode. One of McGoohan's most notable stage experiences had been playing Starbuck in Orson Welles' production of *Moby Dick – Rehearsed*. So the notion of gradually crafting an epic, ambiguous, potentially infuriating work of unique art was not unknown to him.

Certainly *The Prisoner* aspires to be enigmatic. It appears to reach out for multiple interpretations, just as *Moby Dick* might seem to do. Many labels can be attached to it, 'surreal' or 'Kafkaesque' being the most common. This invites the danger that the series will be thought of as having no fixed meaning (other than a vague aspiration to support individuality and 'freedom'). But appearances can be deceiving, especially when a work like *The Prisoner* maintains its own conspiracy of silence against the viewer.

Consider the narrative, as it unfolds. The Prisoner is assigned a number, Number 6, as his only identification in The Village. He rejects this. Presumably he knows his own name. Why, then, does he never in 17 episodes speak it: 'I am not a number – I am a free man! And my name is John Drake/Winston Jones/Whatever'? In *Many Happy Returns* he claims his name is Peter Smith, so unconvincingly that we assume he's lying. In *Do Not Forsake Me* he identifies himself by an alphanumeric code. Why does The Prisoner not insist on using his real name? Why do we never know it?

Similarly, The Prisoner and Number 2, his interrogator, must know what his former job was. So why don't they ever discuss it? In the first episode, *Arrival*, there's a suggestion in the dialogue – not in the script – that Number 6 was once a spy.

Do suggestions of this kind continue?

As the series progresses, what do we learn of Number 6 and of the other prisoners? How many of them were secret agents? How many were something else, entirely?

Who runs The Village? What does the Penny Farthing mean? And what is The Village for? To break and debrief recalcitrant secret agents? Or something else? What does *The Prisoner*, especially in its remarkable last episode, tell us? There are answers to these questions. Let us watch the series, and uncover them.

Since I think viewing the episodes in the sequence in which they were made contributes to understanding the series, I'll view and address them in this order:

1. *Arrival*
2. *Free for All*
3. *Checkmate*
4. *Dance of the Dead*
5. *The Chimes of Big Ben*
6. *Once Upon A Time*
7. *The Schizoid Man*
8. *It's Your Funeral*
9. *A Change of Mind*
10. *The General*
11. *A. B. and C.*
12. *Hammer into Anvil*
13. *Many Happy Returns*
14. *Do Not Forsake Me Oh My Darling*
15. *Living in Harmony*
16. *The Girl Who Was Death*
17. *Fall Out*

By contrast, the original British broadcast running order (the way I first saw them) went like this:

1. *Arrival*
2. *The Chimes of Big Ben*
3. *A. B. and C.*
4. *Free for All*
5. *The Schizoid Man*
6. *The General*
7. *Many Happy Returns*

8. *Dance of the Dead*
9. *Checkmate*
10. *Hammer into Anvil*
11. *It's Your Funeral*
12. *A Change of Mind*
13. *Do Not Forsake Me Oh My Darling*
14. *Living in Harmony*
15. *The Girl Who Was Death*
16. *Once Upon A Time*
17. *Fall Out*

The first US release retained that running order, apart from *Living in Harmony*, which was not screened. Later broadcasts and DVD releases changed the overall order in different ways, though *Arrival* was always first, and *Fall Out* last. According to some sources, *Once Upon A Time* was intended by McGoohan to be the final episode of the first season. When the second season was curtailed, he made it the penultimate episode of the second season, instead. *Once Upon A Time* makes sense here, as it ends with the death of Number 2, and *Fall Out* involves his rebirth. Regardless, *Fall Out* also begins with a long series of flashbacks from *Once Upon A Time*, so the reader/viewer will not suffer if s/he views all the episodes, including this one, in the order suggested.

There are several books dealing with *The Prisoner*, and there will no doubt be more in this, its 50th anniversary year. I've found four to be very useful: Ian Rakoff's *Inside The Prisoner: Radical Television and Film in the 1960s*, *The Official Prisoner Companion* by Matthew White and Jaffer Ali, Rupert Booth's biography of McGoohan, *Not A Number*, and Steven Paul Davies' *The Prisoner Handbook* (for which I wrote a brief introduction). Steven has been particularly helpful, having been kind enough to read this manuscript and offer me his excellent advice. There is also much interesting stuff online, including the *Six of One* and *Unmutual* websites. The screenplays and call sheets are, together with the episodes, the most useful resources of all.

ALEX COX
Tucson, AZ
June 2017

1

Episode One
ARRIVAL

The first episode of *The Prisoner* was scripted by George Markstein and David Tomblin. It was directed by Don Chaffey, who had several features and much TV work to his credit, including some episodes of *Danger Man*. Chaffey was most notable for directing the live action on Ray Harryhausen's films *Jason and the Argonauts* and *One Million Years B.C.* His work is solid, but not interesting or inspired. That is presumably what McGoohan wanted. McGoohan had worked with Orson Welles, and various other talented directors. He and his colleagues chose Chaffey for a reason. Perhaps his selection also pleased Lew Grade.

A pre-title sequence was shot on 28 August 1966, on the Bank Holiday weekend. It shows McGoohan's character speeding down a racetrack in a sports car. Then he's in London, driving past the Houses of Parliament and entering an underground garage. He walks purposefully down a featureless corridor, confronts a bureaucrat seated behind a desk, slams down his letter of resignation, and is gone.

As he drives home, his photograph is xxxxxed over and automatically deposited in a 'resigned' drawer. While he's packing his bags, a pair of men in funeral garb exit a hearse which has been following him. Gas is pumped through the keyhole and he collapses. When he awakes, his room looks the same as ever – but its location has changed. Gone are the London high-rises. It is now situated in The Village.

(There are two versions of *Arrival*. The earlier one – of which a 35mm print was made, and screened for CBS, for journalists and for potential directors – featured main theme music by Wilfred Josephs; the later one, which was broadcast, has the familiar main theme by Ron Grainer. In the first cut, McGoohan's reaction to the sleeping gas and then to his first sight of The Village is quite *broad* in acting terms. In the second version, his performance has been edited in a subtler manner: his acting is more minimal, and thus more effective. The two versions are substantially the same, but for a *Prisoner* enthusiast it's an essential duty to compare and contrast them.)

The Prisoner quickly learns that there is no meaningful information about, and no apparent exit from, The Village. Its inhabitants seem complacent and untrustworthy. They all wear badges with Penny-Farthing bicycles and numbers on them. The phones – cordless phones – are only for calls within The Village: a miniature world with piped muzak on the streets, inane public service announcements and stern weather warnings. Returning to his cottage, The Prisoner finds he has a phone – a black landline bearing the number 6. It rings. 'Is your number Six?'

The Prisoner answers yes, it is. He receives an invitation from Number 2, in the Green Dome, to come to breakfast.

Number 2 (Guy Doleman) is a smooth-faced individual whose look – slightly raffish haircut, blazer, striped white, black and yellow scarf – bespeaks an English public school or 'good' university. In later years, this fellow could be at home in Tony Blair's cabinet, or in Theresa May's. He gives The Prisoner his first clue as to why he has been kidnapped:

NUMBER 2: 'The information in your head is priceless. I don't think you realise what a valuable property you have become. A man like you is in great demand on the open market...

'A lot of people are curious about what lies behind your resignation. You've had a brilliant career. Your record is impeccable. They want to know why you suddenly left.'

NUMBER 6: 'What people?'

NUMBER 2: 'Personally, I believe your story. I think it really was a matter of principle. But what I think doesn't really count. One has to be sure about these things.'

There, in a nutshell, is the conflict of the series. Number 2 is assigned to 'break' The Prisoner – by hook or by crook, to extract vital information from him. As Number 2 readily admits, he doesn't necessarily think this needs to be done. But he is just a cog in a very large wheel, whose opinions don't matter, as we shall see. And The Prisoner, as we shall also see, is apt to resist.

What was The Prisoner's brilliant career?

Projected on Number 2's giant screen are pictures – from The Prisoner's childhood, and photos which seem to be surveillance images. Number 2 mentions a time when he waited for an individual named Chambers. This doesn't appear in the episode's scripts, and seems to be an improvisation of the actors, on-set. What does it mean? Was Chambers a spy, to be turned by our side, or one of our fellows who had to be prevented from defecting? Was he something other than a spy? It isn't clear. The information isn't there. Chambers is mentioned, then he's gone. How did Chambers concern The Prisoner? We are not told. The Prisoner might have been a secret agent. Or he might have been engaged in top-secret, government work. 'The information in your head is priceless...'

To whom is it priceless? As The Prisoner observes, he doesn't know which side Number 2 is working for – the Russians or the British – and he doesn't care. As a matter of principle, he will reveal the time and date of his birth, and no more. He will not even speak his own name.

Number 2 takes The Prisoner for a helicopter ride and displays all the condescension and superciliousness of the English civil servant. He recommends the Citizens Advice Bureau: 'They do a marvellous job. Everybody's very nice.' There is even a Social Club: 'Members only – but I'll see what I can do for you.' The signage encourages the idea of an idyllic retirement community: 'Walk on the grass'. But the illusion is swiftly shattered when Number 2 barks at the strollers in the park, through his megaphone, 'Wait! Be still!' and everyone except The Prisoner freezes in mid-step.

Now the dark side of The Village is revealed, in the form of the floating, hovering weather balloon/beach ball which we will later know as Rover. In the first cut of *Arrival*, Rover appears atop a fountain, then atop a building, then bounces and squirms its way across the plaza, accompanied by menacing and disturbing sounds. The moment is sinister enough. But in the second, broadcast, version, Rover's appearance causes one of the Villagers – a young man with sunglasses – to freak out and attempt to flee. In this cut (using additional footage from the second Portmeirion shoot) Rover pursues and suffocates the youth. We don't know whether the lad has been rendered unconscious or killed, but Rover's physical capacity to crush dissent is very clear.

At the Labour Exchange (the Labour Exchange and Citizens Advice Bureau were real English institutions of the sixties: part of our socialist welfare state, which also provided free health care and, for the lucky ones like me, free university education. In 1966 these things weren't yet science fiction or fantasy) The Prisoner is introduced to a psychologist (or market researcher) who toys with a wooden cogs-and-wheels apparatus and asks him to fill out a questionnaire. Our protagonist smashes the stick-toy and returns to his cottage, only to encounter a fantastically sexy girl in a Luis Buñuel/Jeanne Moreau servant-girl outfit (Stephanie Randall). 'I'm your personal maid,' she says. 'The Labour Exchange sent me.'

Now, McGoohan had a take on his character – indeed, on all the characters he played: that the individual in question didn't get involved, either sexually or romantically, with women. This had been the case with John Drake, in *Danger Man*, and it had served to differentiate his character from James Bond (a role which McGoohan had turned down). But when The Prisoner is confronted by a woman as all-out sexy gorgeous as his *faux* French maid, it's easy to regret the choice the actor made. As he suspects, she is another prisoner, offered her freedom in return for spying on him. And so, she is ejected. Markstein, interviewed after he left the series, said that he had strongly opposed the asexuality of McGoohan's character, which he put down to 'prudishness'. Vincent Tilsley, one of the series' writers, agreed with Markstein. But such was to be the character of The Prisoner, who showed neither love nor affection in any episodes. One can also make a strong case for McGoohan's decision. If The Prisoner were to develop a romantic interest in the Maid, it would be an easier matter for The Village authorities to debrief him (as it were), and future episodes of *The Prisoner* might all be layered with an obligatory 'love interest' sub-plot. In general, the women characters in the series are stronger and more interesting precisely because they weren't expected to fulfil conventional TV roles, and because women actors were frequently cast in roles written for men.

During his remonstration with the failed maid, The Prisoner is distracted by one of the walls – which slides up to reveal a new addition to the cottage, containing bed, kitchen, and lava lamps. In the kitchen cupboards, he finds 'Village Food' in cans bearing the Penny Farthing logo. He destroys his radio – which plays muzak and cannot be turned off – only for The Village to unnerve him further. For the electrician who comes to fix his radio is the exact double of a gardener who he meets moments later. (The actor in question was Oliver MacGreevy.)

Our Prisoner is planning a break for freedom. Yet in the course of less than a day he has also adopted two Village-ish attitudes. Asked 'Is your number Six?' by the operator, he answers 'Yes'. And after reacting with suspicion to the first couple of people who salute him 'Be seeing you!', he volunteers the same salute to the electrician. His first escape attempt gets nowhere beyond fisticuffs with a couple of security men, on the Portmeirion beach, for possession of a Mini-Moke. Mini-Mokes were not invented for *The Prisoner*, though they certainly fit right into its celebration of the miniature, the semi-practical, and the twee. They were 'open air' cars made by the company which manufactured the Mini, and were popular for almost twenty years. I rented them when I lived in Almería, Spain, and they were not great on desert roads, being very low to the ground and apt to shed their exhaust pipes. But a not-very-practical vehicle with a limited range and little off-road capability was an ideal transport for The Village!

Captured by Rover (the second cut of *Arrival* makes his suffocation/incapacitation clearer), The Prisoner is drugged and taken to The Village Hospital. There he wakes to discover a friend from his former life, one Cobb (Paul Eddington), lying in an adjacent bed. Cobb, like The Prisoner, does not know where he is or how he got there. He says he was drugged while on a trip to Germany, woke up here, and has been pumped for information ever since. A doctor takes The Prisoner away for tests, and en route he witnesses, in adjoining corridors, instances of strange, threatening psychological procedures. Tapes and an IBM-type punch card confirm his health is excellent. But in his absence from the ward, Cobb has apparently committed suicide, by throwing himself out of a window.

Given Markstein and McGoohan's interest in matters of spying, parapolitics, and mind control, it's worth mentioning at this point the case of Frank Olson – a CIA operative involved in Agency drug experiments who supposedly threw himself out of a window in 1953. According to the Rockefeller Commission Report, 'Beginning in the late 1940s, the CIA began to study the properties of certain behaviour-influencing drugs (such as LSD) and how such drugs might be put to use in intelligence activities'. The programme was variously known as BLUEBIRD, ARTICHOKE, and MKULTRA. A series of 'in the wild' drug experiments took place, in one of which Olson was slipped a dose of LSD without his knowledge. When he suffered 'serious after-effects' he was sent, with a CIA minder, to see a New York psychiatrist. After five days of observation, Olson killed himself, or was murdered and thrown from a window, in the manner of *The Prisoner*'s Cobb.

The story of Frank Olson didn't become widely known until Freedom of Information requests by the authors John D. Marks and Walter Bowart, in the early 1970s. The Rockefeller Commission Report – officially the President's Commission on CIA Activities Within the United States – was released in 1975, almost a decade after *The Prisoner* was made. Could George Markstein, with his contacts in the world of secret agentry, have heard the story from another source? Someone in the know had told him of the ISRB 'holiday camp' in Scotland. Fascinated by such matters, Markstein may have been privy to other interesting information. If the reference to Olson's fate isn't intentional, it's remarkably synchronicitous.

In 1966 psychedelics were, for most people, unknown. Within a year, they would be famous as recreational drugs and instruments of 'mind expansion'. But the idea that intelligence agencies were experimenting with drugs as mind-control agents, and killing their own people in the process, was beyond astonishing. It was also fantastic material for an innovative TV drama.

After they parted company, McGoohan spoke of *The Prisoner* more as a story of militant individualism, of the right to privacy and to personal integrity; Markstein continued to insist on the espionage angle. And *Arrival* is clearly espionage-tinged. Even if The Prisoner himself is not a spy, he is outrageously the victim of a black operation: kidnapped, and 'rendered', seemingly permanently, into a Potemkin Village inhabited solely by prisoners – broken and unbroken – and by their jailer/interrogators, all acting cheerful, wearing silly hats and capes.

Released from The Hospital, The Prisoner is given four ID cards, a badge saying Number 6, which he discards, and a blazer which he wears until the penultimate episode. He heads for the Green Dome, only to discover a New Number 2 (George Baker) – very similar to the previous version, with same smooth, New Labour/Coalition looks and blazer. This one is a little more brutally frank, less patient with The Prisoner, who he advises will henceforth be known as Number 6.

Here *Arrival* lurches in a new, unnecessary direction. Instead of developing the character of the Maid, which it obviously should, the script has The Prisoner/Number 6 witness what he thinks is the funeral of Cobb, and pursues a woman (Virginia Maskell) who claims to have been his co-conspirator in an escape bid. In the script, she is known as WOMAN, and the Maid as GIRL, which is disappointing when one essays to view the series as a whole: characters should have numbers, damn it! But *The Prisoner* was an organic work of art, its scripts were being written one by one, its concepts developed, its episodes shot, fragmentarily, over many months. The complete world of *The Prisoner* would develop over time... eighteen months of time, and was not, as yet, to be known.

WOMAN claims to have loved Cobb, and to have arranged for his escape by helicopter. She offers the same way out to our protagonist. 'Can you fly a helicopter?' 'I might.' With her aid – even though he knows she is reporting to Number 2 – The Prisoner manages to board the chopper and take off. But after flying a short distance he discovers that he is aboard a drone, operated from Number 2's all-seeing Control Room. Forced to land, The Prisoner is escorted back to The Village by Rover.

In the Control Room, Cobb – who is not dead at all – takes leave of Number 2. His presence in The Village has been a ruse, an early attempt to disorient and extract information from The Prisoner. Now he is returning to the outside world, he remarks, 'Mustn't keep my new masters waiting'. What does he mean? Has Cobb, formerly a British agent, been 'turned' by the Russians and gone to work for them? Or is he simply starting a new job: seconded from GCHQ to NSA, or from MI6 to NATO? In this first script, Markstein and Tomblin keep both options open.

The first cut of *Arrival* ends with The Prisoner knocked down by Rover, as Number 2's Butler marches past, bearing a beach umbrella. In the broadcast version, The Prisoner is tracked by Rover, but not knocked down; we end on the Butler. Observe how Tobias-Shaw's casting changed the Butler's character. In the first draft of the script, he is described as 'very formal but a man obviously in good physical shape who'd be at home in an E-Type Jag'. In the third draft – presumably the shooting script – this description and the Butler's brief dialogue are crossed out. The part had been cast, not with a James Bondish actor, but with the small and striking Angelo Muscat. He, Peter Swanwick, who frequently played the Supervisor in the Control Room/Observation Room, and Fenella Fielding, whose voice provides the public service announcements of the early episodes, can be described as the only series regulars, besides The Prisoner himself.

Another aspect of *Arrival* which may prove illuminating is the music. Twice the score references children's nursery songs: first 'Pop Goes the Weasel', then 'Boys and Girls Come Out to Play'. The two tunes may be meant simply to emphasise the infantile nature of Village life. But the word 'Pop' will take on a certain significance as the series progresses. We shall return to Pop.

WHAT HAVE WE LEARNED?

Kidnapped by unknown parties, The Prisoner may or may not have been a spy. The location of The Village, and the allegiances of those who run it, are entirely unknown.

2

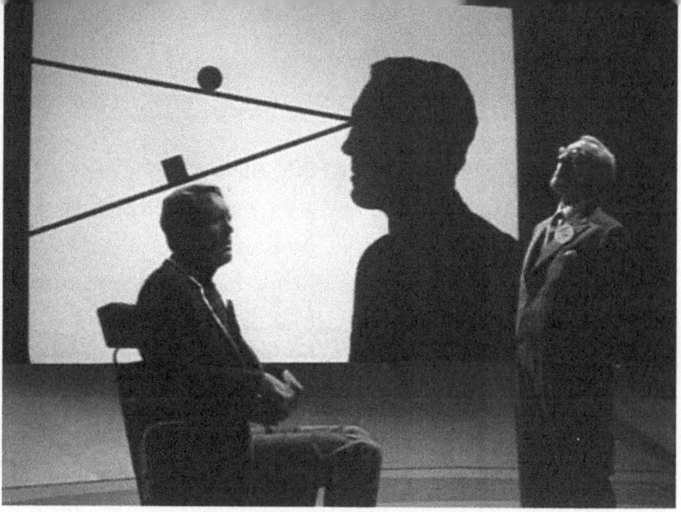

Episode Two

FREE FOR ALL

The second episode filmed, *Free for All*, begins with a shorter cut of the introductory sequence – an exemplary beginning. In a new shot, McGoohan is seen speeding away from Buckingham Palace, a visual surely included to please American buyers. All but two of the subsequent episodes will feature this new montage.

A call sheet records that *Free for All* was being filmed on 15 September, twelve days after the company moved to Portmeirion. *Arrival* had yet to be completed: Jack Shampan was back in London, building its sets at MGM, and the main company was shooting the exteriors of a new episode. The call sheet lists Don Chaffey as director, but this was the second unit: Patrick McGoohan is credited as the director of the finished episode.

That McGoohan should direct an early episode made sense. The actor/producer was intimately involved with the project. He had written *Free for All*'s script, under the pseudonym of Paddy Fitz. And Chaffey had his work cut out for him, with three more episodes to shoot, back-to-back. If he did cede first unit to his star, this suggests a generous nature, and an impressive lack of ego – perhaps the reasons he had been hired.

Free for All is an excellent episode, following *Arrival* admirably. The characters in the first episode were generally fine; the characters here are interesting. The acting in episode one was perfectly good; some of the acting in this episode is outstanding.

The New Number 2 (Eric Portman) invites himself to breakfast at Number 6's residence. Breakfast is wheeled in by a new Buñuel-style maid, Number 58 (Rachel Herbert). Number 2 is amused that Number 58 speaks no English, but confides in Number 6 that he is worried about the coming Village election. 'Some of these good people don't appreciate the value of free elections... they think it's a game.' Number 2 invites Number 6 to run against him. Number 6, immediately interested, asks what will happen if he wins.

NUMBER 2: 'You're the boss.'

NUMBER 6: 'Number 1 is the boss.'

NUMBER 2: 'Should you win Number 1 will no longer be a mystery to you.'

At a political rally, the crowd chants words written on cards displayed by Number 2's Butler: 'Progress! Progress! Progress!' Number 2 introduces Number 6 as 'a recent recruit, not, perhaps, as yet known to all of you, whose outlook is particularly militant and individualistic.' Number 6 rants at the assembled Villagers through his megaphone. They laugh when he declares that he is not a number.

NUMBER 6: 'At some time, in some place, all of you held positions of a secret nature, and had knowledge invaluable to an enemy. Like me, you are here, either to have that knowledge protected or extracted.'

Quickly the crowd turns in his favour. Number 2 applauds him, too. Large placards bearing his face appear. Number 6 is mobbed by confetti-throwing voters, and driven away in a Moke by Number 58. A journalist and photographer – Numbers 112 and 112B – attempt an interview. Number 6 gives no comments, so Number 112 makes the answers up: 'Intends-to-fight-for-freedom-at-all-costs' 'Will-tighten-up-village-security.' The photographer and reporter depart, and the script repeats *Arrival*'s doppelganger moment: Number 6 immediately encounters a newspaper boy, played by the same actor as the photographer (Dene Cooper), who hands him a newly-minted copy of his 'interview' in The Village paper, the *Tally Ho!*

Rover shadows Number 6 to the Town Hall, another vast, circular space where Number 2 occupies an eye-in-the-pyramid throne. From a revolving dais, The Prisoner attempts to question the top-hatted Councillors, but 'immobile as statues' they do not reply. Forced to undergo 'The Test', Number 6 meets the Manager of the futuristic Labour Exchange, a benign older gentleman in a grey morning suit (George Benson), who gives him tea and seeks to gain his confidence.

From the Control Room, Number 2 and the Supervisor remark what an excellent job the Manager is doing: Number 2 observes with pride that he's a product of the Civil Service. A call from a superior causes Number 2 some anxiety. 'Certainly, I'll warn them not to damage the tissue...' With the push of a button, the Manager sends an incapacitating bolt of electricity through Number 6, pinning him to his chair. The Manager applies the

Truth Test: on a big screen, he and the other observers watch Number 6's profile as two lines converge on it. The Manager asks him questions, and two geometric objects – a circle and a square – move towards him. The circle, the Manager observes, indicates a lie, and the square signifies the truth.

As the two shapes merge, the Truth Test concludes, and Number 2 telephones for Number 6's driver. Gradually awakening from the Manager's electroshock mind-reading experiment, The Prisoner, seemingly brainwashed, staggers forward and shakes his hand. 'Thanks for the tea. You will be voting for me, of course.' 'Naturally.' It's a creepy end to a disturbing, fascinating scene.

Back at his cottage, Number 6 and Number 58 grow increasingly close. He watches his speeches on TV and lectures her condescendingly. He teaches her the 'be seeing you' salute, but her mastery of the gesture throws him into shock. Number 6 commandeers her Moke and heads for a jetty where two mechanics are working on speedboats. He steals a speedboat, fights off the mechanics, and heads out to sea. Number 2 pursues him in a helicopter, and Number 6 discovers that the speedboat, too, is a drone, controlled from shore. He is captured and floated back by several Rovers, babbling his campaign speech.

Number 6 returns to the campaign trail, and makes more outrageous promises - 'Winter, Spring. Summer or Fall. They can all be yours at any time.' He personally insults Number 2 on the campaign trail, and shouts at two women in a restaurant when he can't obtain any alcohol. Number 58 leads him to a cave – part of a complex of caverns beneath The Village – where a man tends a still. Number 2 is already here, apparently drunk. Number 6 joins him. Their host, Number 2 reveals, is a 'brilliant scientist. This is his hobby.' On a blackboard behind the still is a mass of chalk diagrams. 'We come down once a week, photograph this stuff and clean it up for him so that he can start on a new lot.'

They sing, and Number 6 collapses on the floor. Suddenly Number 2 is 'steely-eyed and dead cold sober'. He and the scientist discuss the proper drug regimen for the remainder of Number 6's campaign. 'Don't worry. There will be no remembrance. The proportions are exact to take him right through the election.'

Drugged and sedated, Number 6 wins the election by a landslide. Even Number 2 votes for him. Emerging from the polling station, Number 6 finds the voters on the street have fallen silent, indifferent to the result now the election is over. Number 2 leads him by the hand up the hill to the Dome. He leaves Numbers 6 and 58 to enjoy his office, and the two engage in a frenzy of button-pushing, making the chairs rise out of the floor and disappear. Then Number 58 slaps Number 6 across the face, increasingly hard, till he wakes up from his stupor and remembers his plan to liberate The Village. He races to the phone and puts out a general announcement, telling the Villagers that they are free to go. 'I will immobilise all electronic controls... I am in command! Obey me and be free!'

In the script, the Villagers don't hear Number 6's words. 'The loudspeakers play gentle background music' and they go about their business. But in the finished episode, Number 6's call to rebellion plays on all the speakers in The Village. The Villagers hear it, and go about their business.

Attempting once again to flee, Number 6 encounters Rover's mechanics in a cave. Here they are contemplating or worshipping the mysterious enforcer. Number 6 is beaten up, carried back to Number 2's office, and placed on a stretcher. Number 58, formerly his maid and driver, is the New Number 2. She asks him, in perfect English, 'Will you never learn? This is only the beginning.' Number 6, drugged and unconscious, is carried home in a Moke ambulance, and the New Number 2 speaks to the old Number 2, flying out in a helicopter. 'Give my regards to the homeland.'

Free for All is a very funny and disconcerting parable about the failure of democracy in a media-rich but culturally- and intellectually-vapid society. The acting is tremendous, and the characters of Number 2, Number 58, and Number 6 himself, are solidly developed. Number 6 is far from exemplary – taking quickly to the limelight, acting fanatically and obnoxiously, and repeating fatuous clichés. But as he is drugged, electro-shocked, and mind-surveilled (by his bedroom lamp!) he is not in control of his actions.

WHAT HAVE WE LEARNED?

When he harangues the crowd, The Prisoner refers to their 'positions of a secret nature … knowledge invaluable to an enemy.' This could mean they are all former spies. But the bootlegger is a 'brilliant scientist' whose current research – scratched on a blackboard in the cave – is of keen interest to those who run The Village. So not only spies are prisoners here. 'Give my regards to the homeland' doesn't sound like something an English person would say. In adventure-movie terms, these are words we might hear from a German, or a Russian character. So, the New Number 2's goodbye may be a clue as to whose black op this is.

And what are we to make of the ongoing trope (present in both episodes so far) in which one actor plays two different roles, the entrance of one immediately following the exit of the other? It can be treated as a surrealist sight-gag, of course, or as a throwaway homage to the theatre, where actors often play multiple roles. Or is it a plot point? Is The Village in the business of employing identical twins? Or cloning people? Will it occur again? It will.

Part of the debate about the meaning and authorship of *The Prisoner* has to do with the relative contributions of Markstein and McGoohan. Ian Rakoff, who knew them both, feels that the intellectual contribution was Markstein's, and that McGoohan brought instinct and emotion to the project. Rakoff certainly knew that side of McGoohan, whose behaviour sometimes went beyond emotional into the territory of the terrifying. McGoohan was an actor, and actors can be emotional, even nutzoid. But he was also the author of the screenplay *Free for All*, and that is quite an intellectual achievement. The script critiques popular democracy and reveals its protagonist to be a ranter and a demagogue (at least, until his meds kick in). It is well-structured, deals with complex mind-control matters, and has a strong female character. A screenwriter needs emotions, but they must also have an intellect to manage all the structure and dramatic stuff. The screenplay *Free for All* suggests a formidable intellect at work.

The unintelligible language used by Number 58 – meaningless, but dramatically charged – is the first instance of its type in *The Prisoner*. There will be many others, particularly in the scripts written by McGoohan, as we shall see.

3

Episode Three

CHECKMATE

Checkmate began shooting in Portmeirion on 20 September 1966. The script was titled *The Queen's Pawn*. It was written by Gerald Kelsey, and directed by Don Chaffey.

It isn't the first chess reference of the series, nor the last: in *Arrival*, Number 6 played chess with the old admiral, Number 66, and was checkmated. Now, he's invited by an attractive Queen (Rosalie Crutchley) to join the game on a life-size chess board, as her Pawn. He agrees to participate. In a series of unscripted cutaways, as the players move below him, Number 2's Butler plays the game on his own board. Number 6 is an inattentive player, ignoring loudspeaker exhortations to move. He witnesses one of the chess-men, a Rook (Ronald Radd), freak out and make an unauthorised dash across the board.

The hapless Rook is taken to The Hospital for re-education. A rakish and dashing Number 2 (Peter Wyngarde) invites Number 6 to witness the Rook's treatment.

At The Hospital, the Rook is part of a cruel Pavlovian conditioning process, in which he is denied water, electrocuted when he tries to get it, and then ordered to drink from the electrified water cooler. This is supervised by a Psychiatrist (Number 23, icily played by Patricia Jessel) who assures Number 2 that 'from now on he'll be fully cooperative.'

Fortunately, he is not. Number 6 follows the Rook and interrogates him: the Rook confesses that he 'invented a new electronic defence system' and tried to 'share it with the world.' Number 6 enlists the Rook and other Villagers – including another one-actor-in-two-consecutive-service-jobs, the Painter/ Number 42 (Danvers Walker) – and the shopkeeper from *Arrival* (Dennis Shaw), in an escape plot. Simultaneously, the Psychiatrist drugs the compliant Queen and mind-controls her into believing that she loves Number 6 and must follow and report on him to the authorities. Number 6, rather surprisingly, submits to word association tests, after which the Psychiatrist insists to Number 2 that The Prisoner has 'aggressive tendencies. My advice would be leucotomy to knock out these centres of the brain.' Leucotomy is lobotomy, the dreadful, mind-crippling, surgical practice invented by the same medical establishment which brought us Thalidomide and electroshock 'therapy'. That such horrors exist is nothing new. But that they were mentioned in a television entertainment, in the mid-1960s, is astonishing.

Number 6 is saved from compulsory brain surgery by Number 2, who declares him too valuable an asset, at least for now. The Prisoner continues with his new escape plan, stealing electrical equipment so that the Rook can build a radio transmitter. He discovers the Queen's 'emotion generator' – which reports on his proximity to her – and gives it to the Rook. Number 6 and the Rook use the purloined equipment to make a MAYDAY call, claiming to be a downed aircraft. He and the rest of his team stage a raid on the bell tower to put out a searchlight; a Village henchman is hurled from the tower during the fight.

Meanwhile, in the Dome, Number 2 sits cross-legged, wearing a martial arts outfit. A phone call disturbs him, and he shatters a wooden board with a deft karate chop. (The original script has no karate, and describes Number 2 as 'engaged in Yogi exercises'. As in Yogi Bear? Some of the more interesting stuff in this episode isn't in the original screenplay, but in the on-set improvisation of the actors.) Number 6 and his rebel crew overpower Number 2, who makes no effort to use his martial arts skills, and Number 6 goes to see what's happened to their rescuers.

He rows an inflatable out to the ship which has supposedly responded to his MAYDAY call – only to encounter more Village henchmen, and Number 2 on a two-way television connection. Number 2 produces the Rook, who – thinking Number 6 was one of his guards all along – has betrayed their plot to the authorities. Again, Number 6 fights off the heavies for control of the vessel, only to realise that it too is a drone, and that Rover is on its way.

Again, Tobias-Shaw's casting is first-rate. Wyngarde and Jessel are excellent (how fortunate that the casting director and executive producer ignored the script, which has a *male* Psychiatrist), while Radd does the best he can with a miserable role.

WHAT HAVE WE LEARNED?

As the Queen tells The Prisoner, 'That's the trouble here. There's no way of telling who you can trust.' And the episode bears this message out. *Checkmate*, like *Free for All*, features a character who was once a scientist, and is now a prisoner of The Village. Number 6 proves a hard-working assistant to the brilliant electrical engineer, but no electronics expert – he doesn't recognise the value of the transistors in the 'emotion generator'. This is a clue to his profession, as well.

4

4

Episode Four

DANCE OF THE DEAD

Dance of the Dead began in Portmeirion, and was finished on the sound stages at MGM. Anthony Skene was the screenwriter, and Don Chaffey the director. According to Ian Rakoff, an assistant editor on the series, the episode was initially left on the shelf, uncut, till it was claimed by John S. Smith, the principal editor of *The General* and *It's Your Funeral.* Rakoff describes both the latter episodes as incomplete, relying heavily on stock or second-unit footage, whereas *Dance of the Dead* was more finished and, he and Smith felt, contained better material.

While he sleeps, Number 6 is wired by lab-coated doctors to a machine. He receives a telephone call from Dutton (Alan White), a colleague from London, who tells him that the members of their group – he, Dutton, Arthur and the Colonel – must reveal 'all they know' at the behest of an unnamed Committee. Number 6, though under the influence of drugs and electronics, refuses to reveal any secrets. Number 2 (Mary Morris) intervenes and orders the dangerous experiment curtailed. Dutton appears to be a brainwashed automaton under the control of a sinister, bespectacled Doctor (Duncan Macrae).

This Number 2 has a somewhat different agenda from her predecessors, who treated Number 6 with relative kid gloves due to the information he possesses. She insists, 'I don't want him broken. I want him won over. This man has a future with us.' (In the original script, Number 2 is a man who attends the fancy-dress dance as Jack the Ripper. Tobias-Shaw gave us instead another woman Number 2, clad in a fetching Peter Pan outfit.)

Number 6 wakes again to public service announcements and classical muzak. He chats with Number 2 via the television. Surveilled even in his bathroom, he tries to discourage the attentions of a new sexy maid, dressed in a French courtesan outfit. He encounters Number 2's black cat, and witnesses a parade of Villagers celebrating the impending Carnival and Dance. Number 2 hopes he will attend.

NUMBER 2: 'No game is worth playing if you can't win. That's not very English, I know.'

NUMBER 6: 'Are you English?'

She sounds as if she is. But Number 2 won't say. Number 6 tries to invite his Observer – a blonde girl, tasked to spy on him – to the Dance. Highly ideological and suspicious, she will not go.

That night, Number 6 resists all The Village's efforts to make him sleep. An elderly Night Maid offers him a mug of something. The lamp above his head pulses and Number 2's voice urges him to sleep. Number 6 escapes by jumping from his balcony. He heads for the shore, where he is dogged by Rover, and collapses on the beach. The next morning he finds a drowned man, in whose pockets are a wallet, and a radio.

(There follow some plot developments whose utility eludes me. Number 6 steals rope and a life belt and puts his own ID in the dead man's wallet. He also writes a note to the authorities, urging them to investigate, and encloses a hand-drawn map. He then pushes the corpse out to sea.) Dutton, his former associate, confronts him on the beach. Dutton fears he will be rendered brain-dead by The Village's scientist-torturers, who don't believe that he has already told them everything he knows.

Number 6 attempts to find a coherent voice on the dead man's radio, but, as with the radio in Cocteau's *Orphée*, only strange, deadpan poetry emerges. Caught in the act by Number 2, he surrenders the radio. That evening, he attends the fancy-dress ball in the costume assigned to him: his own dinner jacket. Slipping away from the party, he dons a white lab coat and investigates the building. He finds the drowned man in a cabinet in a morgue. Number 2 and her cat appear. She invites him back to the dance, where he is put on trial before three judges, charged with Breaking the Rules. In a scene reminiscent of the travails of Alice in Wonderland, Number 6 faces three judges: Queen Elizabeth/his latest maid (Denise Buckley), Julius Caesar/ the town crier (Aubrey Morris) and Napoleon/the sadistic doctor (Macrae). Like Alice, Number 6 faces some serious adversity. All three judges are strong actors: Morris later played the sinister probation officer, Mr Deltoid, in *A Clockwork Orange*.

Number 6 defends himself, demanding quite reasonably, 'Has anyone ever seen these Rules?' and calling Dutton as a character witness. But Number 2 leads forth a bent and broken figure in a jester's outfit: Dutton, fresh from The Hospital, is a mindless vegetable. Condemned to death and pursued by a ravening mob,

Number 6 flees and finds himself alone with Number 2 and a teletype machine. He thinks he has destroyed the device – his last act of defiance? – but it springs to life again.

WHAT HAVE WE LEARNED?

Dance of the Dead adds to our suspicion that The Village is a foreign operation, targeting British government scientists or intelligence people, and draining them of information. Number 2 speaks a certain type of upper-crust English, yet won't reveal her nationality.

What more have we learned about Number 6? That he's valuable not only for the information he possesses, but for work he can do in the future. We know the names of some of his former colleagues: Dutton, Arthur, and the Colonel. Most significantly, we now know that in terms of spycraft he is a dead loss. His attempt to plant information on a corpse and float it out to sea is confused and doomed to failure. In four episodes, The Prisoner has so far shown no sign of the successful 'tradecraft' of a professional secret agent. The sub-plot involving the dead body may be the work of Markstein, with his enthusiasm for obscure British secret service lore: during World War Two, British Intelligence came up with Operation Mincemeat, to deceive the Nazi high command as to their invasion plans by dumping a corpse, carrying fake papers, on the coast of Spain. The plan was carried out, though, rather like The Prisoner's efforts here, its effectiveness remains unclear.

5

Episode Five

THE CHIMES OF BIG BEN

The Chimes of Big Ben began its Portmeirion shoot on 30 September 1966. It was the last episode Don Chaffey would direct. The script was by Vincent Tilsley. George Markstein had met Tilsley at a Writers' Guild committee meeting; later, he called Tilsley out of the blue, and pitched the project to him. Tilsley was intrigued, and came up with an outline of *The Chimes of Big Ben* the same afternoon. The episode relies very little on its Portmeirion footage. The longer 'exterior' scenes – a piece of seafront, the woods, outside Number 6's house at night – were shot on a sound stage, at MGM.

The episode starts with the New Number 2 (Leo McKern) surveilling Number 6 and marvelling at his sense of humour, a character trait missing from his official file. Long haired, with the manner of an enthusiastic, student-oriented university professor, Number 2 quickly develops a love/hate relationship with The Prisoner. 'I'm glad you're here!' he tells him, only to become upset when Number 6 departs from his personality analysis by unexpectedly adding five sugars to his tea. When he vows to escape, return and destroy The Village, Number 2 adds 'persecution complex amounting to mania; paranoid delusions of grandeur' to Number 6's file. Veering from the benign to the sadistic, he vows to have Number 6 'whimpering'. In his script, Tilsley has Number 6 request a cigarette, then stub it out on the back of his hand, to show Number 2 how unlikely this whimpering is to occur. But it seems the scene wasn't shot, perhaps due to increasing concern about cigarette advertising, and the portrayal of tobacco, on British TV.

Nadia Rakowski (Nadia Gray), a new Russian arrival, is helicoptered in, unconscious. Number 2 and Number 6 watch via surveillance camera as Nadia wakes in a replica of her room at home and discovers she is in The Village. Number 6 is suspicious of her when they meet, but she persists in using her own name and rejecting the number – 8 – which she has been assigned. She claims she too has resigned from a top-secret position. Number 6 is stung when Nadia assumes he is Number 2's assistant, pumping her for information. Yet Number 2 and Number 6 become unusually friendly. Next day, they both enjoy a collegial conversation beneath a beach umbrella. In the script, Number 6 shrugs when Number 2 asks if he may join him; but in the scene McGoohan warmly welcomes McKern to the table. All the while, Nadia seemingly wrestles with her options, and attempts to swim for freedom.

NUMBER 6: 'Has it ever occurred to you you're just as much a prisoner as I am?'

NUMBER 2: 'But my dear chap, of course! I know too much. If I wasn't in the Village they'd have to send me here. We're both lifers.'

Number 2 observes that it doesn't matter which side runs The Village – the West or the East – since they are mirror images, and the owners of The Village have created an ideal, international community here.

NUMBER 2: 'A perfect blueprint for World Order...'

NUMBER 6: 'All the earth one big Village.'

NUMBER 2: 'That is my hope. What's yours?'

NUMBER 6: 'To be the first man on the Moon.'

Nadia's escape attempt is thwarted by Rover. Number 2 asks Number 6 to join him at The Hospital, where Nadia is apparently being subjected to high-tech torture. Sitting in a chair for 18 hours straight, she is, per Number 2, supposed to figure out a way to escape a windowless room with an electrified floor. Instead, she appears to attempt suicide, at which point Number 2 calls off the experiment. To save Nadia from further cruelty, Number 6 agrees to 'collaborate', by taking part in an arts and crafts exhibition.

In the script, Nadia is assigned the job of Number 6's latest foxy maid. In the episode, there is no suggestion of any maid-work for Nadia: Number 6 and Number 8 just hang out together, and grow increasingly close. Though this is not close as you or I might know it: Number 6 fakes romance so as to fool Number 2's surveillance cameras, while plotting their escape and reassuring Nadia as to her future relationship with Her Majesty's Government. With the exception of the contradictory *Do Not Forsake Me* episode, this is the closest Number 6 will come to a relationship, romantic or otherwise. Nadia is smart and beautiful, but she interests Number 6 because she claims to know the location of The Village, which, she says, is in Lithuania. The two make plans to escape, via sea to Poland, and thence to England. Denied the use of chisels, saws or axes for his art exhibit, Number 6 fabricates wood and stone tools, fells a tree, and builds a collapsible sailing boat which he convinces Number 2 and the other Villagers is an abstract art piece. The art exhibition is Number 2's pet project: all the other entries in the contest are paintings, sculptures, or tapestries depicting him. (The work of designer Jack Shampan, in the variety he provided of not-very-good drawings, sketches, busts, etc. of Leo McKern as Number 2, for this ridiculous art exhibit, is to be applauded. Shampan repurposed his ubiquitous circular MGM set for the exhibition room where the numerous homages to Number 2 are on display.)

Delighted that Number 6 is involved, Number 2 leans heavily on the judges, who award his incomprehensible entry first prize – even though it lacks a likeness of Number 2. (This scene is one of director Chaffey's best – his lighting is always bright, focus sharp, acting on the money, and he creates a fine critical commentary on art-world pretentiousness and its dependence on state or corporate *largesse.*)

Having given a modest acceptance speech ('Spoken like a true artist!'), Number 6 donates his prize, 2,000 Work Units, to Number 38, creator of a tapestry featuring Number 2. He and Nadia head for the shore, assemble the boat, and using the tapestry as a sail, depart. (The VFX shot of them at sea, beneath Number 2's billowing likeness, is particularly fine.) They are pursued by Rover, but Nadia has a confederate waiting on a Polish headland: his rifle obliges Rover to retreat. It looks like Nadia is on the level, as her confederate has arranged their transit to London in a wooden box. Number 6 gives

Nadia a written message: 'Ask him to transmit this to London immediately. He will not understand it. It is in code. It is a delivery note.' He asks the man for his watch, so that he can time their journey, by road, sea and air. It should take 16 hours.

The Prisoner and Nadia undertake an uncomfortable journey, nailed inside separate compartments of the box. She is increasingly flirtatious, calling him 'Big Ben'. He times their trip meticulously: when the box is finally opened, they are apparently in his London office, being greeted by an old friend, Fotheringay (Richard Wattis), and another Civil Service mandarin, Colonel J (Kevin Stoney). One of the best scenes of the series follows, in which the Colonel attempts to debrief The Prisoner, demanding to know why he resigned. The Prisoner grows suspicious. Colonel J claims to know nothing about any Village, and insists that The Prisoner must come clean: he is the one who quit, then disappeared, then turned up behind the Iron Curtain asking to get out. Why did he resign? The familiar chimes of Big Ben sound. The Prisoner looks at his watch. It is eight o'clock. There are eight chimes. As Poland and London are an hour apart, in different time zones, he now knows he has been tricked. To Colonel J's dismay, he traces some wires to a cupboard, in which a hidden tape recorder has been playing the steady hum of London traffic, and the chimes of Big Ben. The Prisoner walks down a corridor and exits the building. He is back in The Village (though this is actually a set built for an American war movie, *The Dirty Dozen*, on the backlot of MGM Studios, with Portmeirion-style dressing and costumes). Number 2 tells Fotheringay to return to London and await instructions. Number 6 salutes Nadia, one of the plotters, and walks away.

WHAT HAVE WE LEARNED?

The location of The Village is still unknown. It might be in Lithuania, near Poland. Or it might not. Ownership of The Village seems increasingly unclear. Number 2 has thrown it into doubt, and questioned whether it even matters. And, like it or not, Number 6 is increasingly identified *with* The Village, rather than against it: the Rook assumed he was a Village agent, and Nadia claims to believe that he is Number 2's assistant. This is, perhaps, a failing on his part: surrender to the temptation of the 'position of authority' that Number 2 offered him in *Arrival.* It's also part of The Village's plan to subvert him, and break him down. Yet, in these early episodes, while The Prisoner takes an active role in Village life, it's always with escape in mind.

In *The Chimes of Big Ben*, Number 6 proves excellent with his hands. He's a remarkable carpenter, able to build a sailing vessel with handmade tools. This is no ordinary feat, even if Number 6 was 'top of his class in woodwork at the age of 15'. It's far beyond the revealed capacities of James Bond, who could order up a mean martini and kill with gun, hand, or knife, but never chopped down trees with a stone axehead, nor scratch built a boat.

Number 6 also reveals his ambition. As his interactions with the Number 2s are usually ironic or angry, we may assume he's being ironic when he remarks, 'I want to be first man on the Moon'. Number 2 laughs, as if this is funny. Perhaps it's meant that way. Perhaps it's a jokey reference to *The Greatest Man in the World*, a highly-successful TV drama in which McGoohan had played exactly that – the first man to land a spacecraft on the Moon (he also played a Russian cosmonaut, in the Armchair Theatre production *The Man Out There*). Let me suggest a third possibility: that Number 6 means what he says. I shall return to this.

The Chimes of Big Ben was chosen as the second episode when the series was broadcast. Perhaps the presence of Richard Wattis as Fotheringay was a comfort to the broadcaster: Wattis had played secret agent John Drake's boss in *Danger Man*. The scene in which Fotheringay responds to a telephone call about The Prisoner's imminent arrival makes no logical sense: Fotheringay is part of a scheme to recreate The Prisoner's London office and get him to divulge his secrets. Why would he play-act his role before The Prisoner arrived? It sets up the arrival well, and convinces us that Fotheringay is on the level, but on a second viewing it's dramatically dodgy.

Lastly, let us praise the Buñuelian weirdness of having The Prisoner and Nadia nailed into separate sections of a wooden box, and playing the series' lightest and sexiest scenes therein, on either side of a plank wall.

6

Episode Six

ONCE UPON A TIME

Degree Absolute – the original title of *Once Upon A Time* – was shot entirely at MGM. There's some b-roll of Number 6 in The Village, but Leo McKern – the first actor to repeat the role of Number 2 – never visited Portmeirion. The total shoot was a short one – eight or nine days – and extremely demanding of the actors. McKern found McGoohan confrontational and miserly. Interviewed years later, he called him 'a dreadful, impossible bully. Always shouting about saving money.' At one point McKern collapsed in his dressing room. Doctors were called, and he was gone for three days. Shooting continued in his absence, with a double. McGoohan was an intense and very particular actor, who could get physical in fight scenes. But as McKern remarked, with hindsight, 'that was great fun… even the agony'. This is why directors love actors!

The episode was written and directed by McGoohan, without a pseudonym. It was clearly written with the cast in mind – the generic Butler is gone; instead Angelo Muscat's character is called 'Angelo'. Rover – described for the first time as a giant sphere – has become part of Number 2's domestic life, and, like a dog who won't get off the sofa, occupies his round, revolving chair.

Very quickly the script veers from generic narrative to experimental drama, as Number 2 – determined to break/understand/dominate Number 6 – watches clips from *Arrival*, *Free for All* and *Dance of the Dead*, and obtains permission from his superiors for a 'Degree Absolute'. Number 2 starts talking to the Supervisor in numbers, whose meaning is unknown, while Number 6 writhes in his sleep on the big screen.

NUMBER 2: 'Blow up Channel 3.'

SUPERVISOR: 'Channel 3. Channel 3.'

NUMBER 2: 'Check profundity.'

SUPERVISOR: '1, 2, 5, 4, 5, 3. First waveband clear.'

NUMBER 2: 'Repeat and increase.'

SUPERVISOR: '1, 2, 5, 4, 5, 3. Still clear.'

NUMBER 2: 'Third waveband. Slow. And hold on 5.'

SUPERVISOR: '1, 2, 5, 4, 3. 5, 5, 5, 5, 5...'

In Number 6's cottage, Number 2 lulls him with nursery rhymes, and the hypnotising lamp works on his slumbering brain. Next morning, The Prisoner awakes in a child-like state, and Number 2 offers to take him for 'walkies'. The Butler conveys him in a wheelchair to the Dome. Number 6 appears to have suffered a mental regression and can be led by the hand, eating an ice cream. All three descend on one of the office's elevator platforms to a moving walkway underground, and thence to a bunker in which Number 2 will attempt to extract The Prisoner's secrets. McGoohan's script describes it thus:

> 'He leads P into the room which is circular in shape, entirely shrouded in black velvet except for one section, being the steel bars of a cage. The main area is lit from above by hanging lamps of great intensity creating pools of light in the principal action areas. There is a see-saw. Large... A swing. Large. A rocking horse. Large. A play-pen. Normal. A go-kart. A desk. A blackboard. A free-standing wardrobe. Two bicycles. Two mini-tractors... an electric organ. Angelo is in the play-pen. The cage is the size of a 23ft caravan, and beyond the bars is set out with all the accoutrements of a luxury one-room self-contained dwelling.'

Such a vivid and specific scene description suggests to me another title for the episode: *Method Actors Go For It!* And, within its lively confines, they certainly do. The acting of all three men is fervent and intense. Number 2, playing the roles of Number 6's schoolmaster, his boxing coach, his fencing master, his bomber pilot, his government employer, and a magistrate, lectures him on the need to conform and attempts to pry the secret of his resignation from him in a series of imaginary encounters. Despite the drugs, hypnosis, and face-to-face head-tripping, Number 6 resists. He plays an honourable schoolboy and a cynical-naive job applicant in scenes which anticipate Lindsay Anderson and Malcolm McDowell's work in *If....* and *O Lucky Man!* He boxes, fences, resists Number 2's demands to be impaled, and apparently relives his past life as a bombardier, and as a prisoner of war who will reveal only his national service number. Almost a week passes as Number 2 and Number 6 play mental word and number games. When he tries to strangle Number 2, Number 6 is knocked unconscious and subjected to more hypnosis. The Butler gives Number 2 a head massage, but sides with Number 6 when – with five minutes of their confinement left – The Prisoner turns the tables on his interrogator and locks him in the cage.

Much of what could be standard TV dialogue is dropped, in lieu of nursery rhymes or repeated number sequences. In his *Prisoner Handbook*, Steven Davies quotes a two-page dialogue exchange between Number 2 and The Prisoner, equal parts dramatic and insane, focusing on numbers and the word 'Pop'. When Number 6 says, 'Pop protect', Number 2 responds 'Protect other people'. But The Prisoner will go no further down that road.

The climax features a numeric countdown, intoned by Number 6: '47 – 46 – 45 – 44' Dropping 'meaningful' dialogue in lieu of lists of numbers, or word-association games, is similar to what McGoohan did in the previous episode he wrote and directed, *Free for All*. There, the characters of Number 58 and Number 2 communicated in an imaginary foreign language. Words are disposable, the writer/director seems to be saying to the actors, and the audience: emotion and intention are everything.

After the countdown, Number 2 lies dead, the door opens and the Supervisor appears. He congratulates The Prisoner, and remarks that they will need the old Number 2's body 'for evidence'. Like the Butler, the Supervisor treats Number 6 as the New Number 2, and asks for instructions. The Prisoner asks to see Number 1, and the Supervisor replies, 'I'll take you'.

Once Upon A Time is an excellent, if pretentious, episode. Sometimes the framing is splendidly extreme, with the faces of Numbers 2 and 6 jammed together in big double closeups. I find the 'black box' environment too low-budget, Equity-waiver theatrical, to do the series full justice, and McGoohan's script does seem a self-conscious attempt to enter the experimental-theatre world of Edward Bond or Samuel Beckett, with some Shakespeare thrown in. Rakoff quotes Lindsay Anderson on that director's only meeting with McGoohan, in which the actor excoriated a production of Beckett's *Endgame* at the Royal Court Theatre. So McGoohan was well aware of the respectable outer limits of the theatre, and apt to have a go himself, within the expansive format of *The Prisoner*. The experiment is very entertaining: as a director, he creates considerable tension via nonsense dialogue, playing with the viewer's expectations and employing skilful visual montage. Today, such an approach would still be rare, perhaps encountered in the further reaches of a film festival. In the late 1960s, such things on television were simply unknown.

WHAT HAVE WE LEARNED?

A great deal, though its meaning may not yet be clear. Number 6's answers to the question, 'Why did you resign?', while still brief, are longer than any previous responses. He says his resignation is a 'state secret', and that he quit, 'For peace... for peace of mind... because too many people know too much.' In his attempt to crack him, Number 2 tries to make Number 6 embrace killing. He revisits The Prisoner's wartime experiences – assuming they are real, and not a hypnosis-induced fantasy – telling him, 'In the war you killed', and Number 6 doesn't deny it. Drugged into believing he's applying for a job as a banker, Number 6 confides in Number 2, 'I was always very good at mathematics.' He is hired, then told his job is a cover for 'secret work... top secret, confidential job'.

If McGoohan intended *Once Upon A Time* to end the first, thirteen-part season, the Supervisor's promise leaves *The*

Prisoner with a tremendous cliffhanger. In the late 1970s I bought, in a used book store in Hollywood, an ITC 'story information' booklet, designed to promote a thirteen-part first season: it lists *Once Upon A Time* as the final episode. When the decision was made to cap *The Prisoner* at 17 episodes, *Once Upon A Time* was rescheduled as the penultimate show. It is, after all, the ongoing story of the Number 2 who claimed to be a prisoner of The Village, and who both admires and detests Number 6. Apparently he lied when he told Number 6, in *The Chimes of Big Ben*, that he too was a prisoner. In *Once Upon A Time* he remarks to his superiors, on the telephone, 'You brought me back here.' Number 2 has a day job elsewhere (in *Fall Out*, we shall learn what it is), and has returned to The Village as part of the ongoing effort to break The Prisoner. When he telephones the cottage, Number 6 replies, 'I know your voice.' 'I've been here before,' Number 2 agrees.

Let's return to the Supervisor's response, when Number 6 asks to see Number 1. 'I'll take you.' He does not say 'to him', nor 'to her'. This follows Number 2 in *Free for All* promising that Number 1 will 'no longer be a mystery'. Usually, in each episode, Number 2 talks to a superior by telephone. But that person is never addressed as Number 1, and so far there's been no suggestion that Number 1 is a person. If not a person, what is Number 1? Presumably something that Number 6 was knowledgeable about, perhaps intimately connected to – even if he did not know it by that number.

7

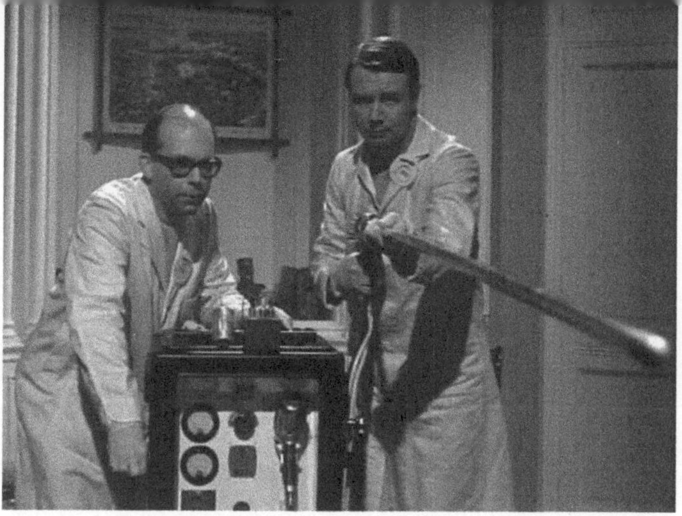

Episode Seven

THE SCHIZOID MAN

The seventh episode, shot over Christmas and the New Year 1966/1967 at MGM (there is one aerial shot of Portmeirion), was scripted by Terence Feely and directed by Pat Jackson. Feely had written for episodic TV dramas like *The Avengers* and *The Saint*; he was to write another *Prisoner* episode and would become a co-director, with McGoohan and Tomblin, of Everyman Films. Jackson had directed films and TV shows, none of them notable. He would direct four episodes. His work is entirely competent, never especially exciting. *The Prisoner*, remarkable in so many ways, is also notable for its conservative, even plodding taste in directors. In his favour, as Jackson observed, he worked fast – producing 5.5 to 6 edited minutes every shooting day: double the ratio a feature film director would be expected to achieve. The ability of Jackson and Chaffey to meet *The Prisoner*'s exacting schedule was an achievement in itself. And episodic drama is a producer's medium – so as long as the executive producer/star retained his intense focus and enthusiasm, extraordinary drama would continue to result.

In *The Schizoid Man*, we're in the territory of contemporary science fiction: the episode feels like a short story by Philip K. Dick. The date is 10 February. Number 6 has become involved – platonically, of course – with an attractive young telepath, Number 24 (Jane Merrow). The New Number 2 (Anton Rodgers) watches as she intuits the contents of cards picked by The Prisoner. Number 2 has a plan to break Number 6, and sets it in motion that same night. According to Feely, in his screenplay Number 24 was Number 6's lover, and able to recognise him via a kiss. Since McGoohan refused to consider any on-screen romantic action, after a fierce argument Feely came up with the idea he called the 'mind-meld'.

'Pulsato!' Number 2 calls out. 'Visual! Oral!' The round lamp which hangs over The Prisoner's bed descends and, as it has done in the past, proceeds to hypnotise and tranquilise him. While he sleeps, technicians shoot him up with drugs and carry him away. For an unknown period of time, he is confined, drugged, to a hospital bed, and tortured with electroshock aversion therapy designed to make him left-handed. He grows a moustache and his hair is dyed. Under hypnosis, he is programmed to believe that his favourite food is flapjacks, and his preferred cigarette a black Russian. He is told repeatedly that he is Number 12.

Number 6 wakes in a different room in The Village – the date is still 10 February. On the street, people address him as Number 12. Number 2 invites him over. The inevitable breakfast ritual takes a sinister turn as Number 6 loads up on flapjacks, and Number 2 tasks him, as his old friend Number 12 – an intelligence agent – to impersonate Number 6.

NUMBER 2: 'When he begins to doubt his own identity, he'll crack. What do you think of the idea?'

NUMBER 6: 'I think it has distinct possibilities. But I'll take quite a lot of convincing I'm not Number 6.'

NUMBER 2: 'Of course! Excellent, Number 12. Always the professional. You've started living the part already.'

Number 2 takes Number 6 back to 'his' cottage where he encounters an impostor who resembles him exactly, and who claims to be Number 6. This is a particularly fiendish Village strategy – and perhaps the most likely to succeed. Number 6 is forced to identify with the number he has rejected, indeed to fight for possession of it. His willingness to do this is particularly strange. Throughout the series, other characters retain their names and insist on using them: Cobb, Dutton, Nadia. In this episode, Number 24 goes by the name of Angela. Whereas The Prisoner clings steadfastly, not to his own name, which remains unspoken, but to the numerical designation his kidnappers have assigned him – just as, in *Free for All,* he sported a rosette bearing the number 6. Seemingly accepted as Number 12, he even forgets the prisoner's primary directive: to escape. Instead, he challenges the false Number 6 to a series of contests, to establish which of them is genuine.

The showdown does not go well. In the 'Recreation Hall' (a Norman church building on the MGM backlot), Number 6 loses a target-shooting and fencing contest with the impostor. They fight and – disabled by his electroshock conditioning – Number 6 fails at fisticuffs, as well. Rover intervenes and escorts both of them back to the Dome. There, Number 2 appears to torture the impostor, and The Prisoner insists that Angela is the one person who can – telepathically – identify him. But Angela is working for The Village: his attempt to 'mind-meld' with her fails, while the impostor enjoys a 100% success rate. The false Number 6 exits, escorting Angela.

That night, The Prisoner is wracked by nightmares. When he wakes in Number 12's room, his clock says it's 10 February, again. But a blood-blister under one of his fingernails – which has seemingly moved a half inch overnight! – jolts The Prisoner into consciousness. He recalls the sadistic conditioning he has undergone, and deliberately electrocutes himself, thereby restoring the primacy of his right hand.

Knocking out two toughs and evading Rover, Number 6 confronts the impostor. The latter menaces him with a deadly nerve gas gun, and reveals that his real name is Curtis. Both seem to have been betrayed by The Village, having been given passwords which don't work – 'Gemini' and 'Schizoid Man'. When the impostor tries to use his password to evade Rover, he is killed. Seizing his chance, Number 6 convinces Number 2 that he is Curtis, and that The Prisoner is dead. He insists on leaving, and Number 2 arranges a helicopter. But, uncertain whether he has the right man, Number 2 plays an old trick on Number 6, asking 'Curtis' to remember him to one 'Susan'. Number 6 falls for the gag – Susan is dead, of course – and the helicopter returns him to The Village.

The Schizoid Man is a strong, well-crafted episode. McGoohan plays both Number 6 and the impostor. There is some fine matte work and over-the-shoulder doubling, in the style of *The Parent Trap*. Today it's relatively easy to double-up the same actor in the frame: everything is possible with software. But in 1966 the *Prisoner* effects crew were shooting on film, and taking their visual effects to the lab as composite mattes – it was the same, expensive, feature-film technology that their neighbours at MGM, the crew of *2001: A Space Odyssey*, were using for their multi-layered shots of spacecraft and the surface of the Moon.

The focus on smoking materials is surprising. Up until now there has been no smoking in The Village (which officially also operates a no-alcohol policy). Suddenly in this episode Number 6's preferred brand of smokes becomes an issue; and his conditioning seems to have left him allergic to cigars. At one point he breaks apart one of the 'black Russian' cigarettes and – in extreme closeup – discovers a wire inside. The mystery is not developed, and cigarettes are rarely seen in later episodes.

WHAT HAVE WE LEARNED?

We don't see much of The Village since the episode was shot at MGM, using the backlot and the recreated stage exterior of Number 6's place. What Villagers we do encounter act according to Number 2's new game plan – that it is still 10 February, and that Number 6 is Number 12. This suggests, not for the only time in the series, that The Village exists purely and simply as an environment for breaking Number 6's will, and that *all* the Villagers are in on the game – either jailers play-acting or prisoners who are entirely compliant. And, unique to *The Schizoid Man*, there are black people in The Village! A Sikh Villager addresses Number 6 as Number 12, and a black operative in the Control Room remarks, 'In Haiti we would say they have stolen his soul.'

When Number 6 – pretending to be Curtis – and Number 2 debrief, in his office, the following exchange occurs:

Number 2: '... we've been in scrapes before, but we've never fallen out over it. The General's not going to behead you.'

Number 6: 'No – well, I won't know until I've reported to him, will I?'

Number 2: 'Report to the General. That's a new one.'

Number 6: 'I don't mean report to him personally. I mean – oh, for Pete's sake, you know what I mean.'

But does he? We've watched this Number 2, like all his predecessors, talk to a superior or superiors by telephone. But they are clearly not the General. Implicit is the notion that the General, like Number 1, is something other than human. Number 6's suggestion that he might report personally to this entity has made Number 2 suspicious. Because the General is not a man, as we shall see.

This complex episode also pays off the mysterious 'dual character' gags of the first three episodes. We learn here that those who run The Village have the capacity to alter the physical characteristics of its inmates, and to replicate their appearances. So the Electrician and Gardener in *Arrival* weren't twins: they were, apparently, clones. The process isn't addressed in *The Schizoid Man*, but we can presume that Curtis, who pretends to be Number 6, didn't always look exactly like Patrick McGoohan. He has been surgically or chemically altered, by a sinister process in the hands of an ever more competent and malevolent power.

According to Rakoff, Lindsay Anderson disliked the kitschy visuals and brightly-coloured costumes of *The Prisoner*. But I think that this very twee atmosphere is essential to what the series is getting at. This isn't *1984*, where a grim, hate-filled environment permits torture, murder and mind control. Anyone can criticise or disapprove of a society like that. But *The Prisoner* was broadcast in the year of the Summer of Love: what of a brighter-coloured, more optimistic, happier environment which permits torture, murder and mind control? Could such places exist? Could England be one of them?

Lastly, though it isn't scripted, we appear to be told that the descending hypnosis lamp above The Prisoner's bed, which regularly puts him into a deep sleep, is named 'Pulsato'.

8

Episode Eight

IT'S YOUR FUNERAL

Most of *It's Your Funeral* was shot over two weeks, at MGM, in January 1967. It was considered a problematic episode by all involved. The script, by Michael Cramoy, was scheduled to be directed by Robert Asher, an old friend of McGoohan, and veteran of light comedy films. Asher confessed to Derren Nesbitt, the actor playing Number 2, that he couldn't understand what it was about. Nesbitt felt the same way. McGoohan and Markstein showed Asher the first print of *Arrival*, which confused him even more. McGoohan fought with Asher on set and alienated some of his co-stars in the process; Asher was fired and McGoohan, uncredited, took over the show. John S. Smith, the editor, felt there wasn't enough material to make a coherent episode. His assistant, Rakoff, wrote that Cramoy had been given a terrible assignment: to write a script based around existing stock material. (It's unclear what this was: presumably the shots of McGoohan's double walking around Portmeirion, and extras listening to loudspeakers, and marching with placards, were shot a couple of months later, in the second Portmeirion visit.) It all sounds hopeless, yet it wasn't. *It's Your Funeral* came together in the cutting room, and in its finished form is tightly-scripted and well-paced. There's no science fiction here: just a fast-moving thriller about intrigue and betrayal within the upper ranks of The Village, and Number 6's efforts to thwart a murder plot.

'Young' Number 2 (Nesbitt, with bleached-blond hair and chunky black spectacles, looking for all the world like a *Thunderbirds* puppet or Joe 90) and the Supervisor observe Number 6 as he is visited by an attractive blonde woman, Monique (Annette Andre). Number 6 assumes she is an agent and tries to throw her out. Under the influence of Number 2's drugs, she collapses and, as anticipated, Number 6 is moved to help her. Upon recovery, Monique tells him she wants to prevent a political assassination, being plotted by a group called the 'jammers'. Refusing to trust her, Number 6 sends her on her way.

Number 2 and his staff track The Prisoner's activities; after a chess game, Number 6 goes to the Recreation Hall for a game of Koshu (a martial art apparently invented by McGoohan, involving two trampolines, crash helmets, boxing gloves and a miniature swimming pool). During the protracted scene of bouncing and tussling, Number 100 (Mark Eden) – pink-blazered henchman to Number 2 – steals Number 6's watch from the locker room, replacing it with a dud. This sends Number 6 to the clock shop – where he spots the detonation mechanism for a bomb on the workbench of an old watchmaker (Martin Miller). Unknown to Number 6, Number 100 is also there – masquerading as one of the conspirators in an assassination plot.

Back in the Green Dome, the acting Number 2 has authorised 'Plan Division Q' which sanctions the assassination. His assistant is worried that the plan 'is still murder' but young Number 2 is pleased with its progress. Number 6, learning that Monique is the watchmaker's daughter, confronts the old rebel and warns that The Village authorities may take heavy reprisals against the entire community. The watchmaker, unmoved and ideologically determined, returns to his bomb-making. Number 6, as Number 2 has predicted, hurries to advise Number 2 that his life is in danger.

As in *Free for All* and *The Schizoid Man*, Number 6 is again doing The Village's work for it: he has now become a secret policeman for the enterprise. But Number 2 is unmoved and ungrateful: he says he knows all about the plot, and that the watchmaker is on his list of malcontents – a list with Number 6's name at the very top. He insists everything is under control, while surreptitiously filming their encounter.

When Number 6 returns to attempt a second warning, he encounters a different Number 2 – the 'old' version, one day away from his retirement. The retiring Number 2 (Andre Van Gyseghem), who also has bleached-blond hair, in less profusion, shows Number 6 a film his successor Number 2 has put together, in which Number 6 appears to be a serial threatener, making identical death threats on camera to three different Number 2s. Number 6 departs, not bothering to make the case that the footage has been doctored. But soon the retiring Number 2 intuits, from the insubordination of his assistants, that Number 6 is right, and that there is an in-house plot to execute him tomorrow, on The Village's 'Appreciation Day'.

It's Your Funeral contains one of the best depictions of The Village bureaucracy. To a twenty-first century reader/viewer, the story doesn't seem so hard to understand. The Village is a place of *extraordinary rendition*, as the process of kidnapping and interrogation abroad has come to be known. Its controllers are capable of evil acts of mind control and extrajudicial killing. So a 'false flag' operation in which an expendable bureaucrat is murdered may indeed be something these controllers want – to justify a violent clampdown, or to promote a new mind control project. Possibly, to English actors and directors in 1966 this seemed an obscure notion. It seems less mysterious today. And, even though he didn't know what he was doing, Derren Nesbitt played his role very well – sniping at the Supervisor for 'slapdash improvisations', suborning his predecessor's assistants, fawning on the phone to his superiors. Meanwhile, the 'old' Number 2 proves himself the perfect Villager. Apprised of his fate, he wearily accepts it:

NUMBER 2: 'Preventing only means postponing. You still don't understand us, Number 6. We never fail. Anyway, why should you care what happens to me?'

NUMBER 6: 'I don't. But innocent people will be blamed.'

NUMBER 2: (genuinely) 'Yes. I'm sorry. There's nothing I can do.'

Faced with such a lame nemesis, Number 6 must take control. He pursues the watchmaker to the bell tower, and relieves him of his bomb detonator. He fights Number 100 for control of the device, which he delivers, in the nick of time, to the old Number 2. The bomb has been planted in Number 2's 'Great Seal of Office', so his predecessor is safe to depart The Village by helicopter.

Number 6, content to see him go, makes no escape attempt.

WHAT HAVE WE LEARNED?

Not much, in terms of advancing our understanding of The Village, its origin, ownership and purpose; nor about why The Prisoner is imprisoned there. *It's Your Funeral* is simply an exciting story of political intrigue. (We can at least observe that, financially, The Village seems to have transferred Work Units to credit cards – which are mechanically punched by the service provider. Twice, in this episode, Number 6 pays for goods or services this way.)

Regarding the character of The Prisoner, *It's Your Funeral* clearly establishes certain things. Faced with a situation where violent action may lead to unknown reprisals, Number 6 vehemently opposes the assassination plot. He attempts to dissuade the watchmaker – a lone conspirator manipulated by a state agent – from his bomb scheme. When that fails, he makes three trips to the Green Dome to alert and update Number 2 about the plot. He's willing to act as an undercover agent for The Village administration – which he supposedly despises – in order to prevent violent recriminations against the Villagers. Despite the fact that almost all the Villagers he's met appear to be double agents or Mata Haris, The Prisoner is still concerned for their wellbeing.

The watchmaker makes the case for violence thus: 'Perhaps it's what they need to wake them up. To shake them out of their lethargy. To make them angry enough to fight.' Number 6 disagrees. At this point in the series, despite the odd punch-up, our hero has seemingly opposed violence which may result in death. Remembering that these episodes were shot in 1967, I want to propose two rock'n'roll alternatives as a way of looking at the conflicting values of a change-oriented time, and to position *The Prisoner* – halfway through the first season – in one of these camps.

The first alternative is posited by The Beatles in their song *Revolution*, specifically in the lines, 'But when you talk about destruction / Don't you know that you can count me out.' The second alternative is that of Thunderclap Newman, who a couple of years later wrote another song called *Revolution*, only to rename it *Something in the Air*. The latter called outright for armed insurrection against authority: 'Break out the arms and ammo / Because there's something in the air...' In January 1967, shooting *It's Your Funeral*, McGoohan and *The Prisoner* were clearly in The Beatles' camp. Before the end of the year, they would anticipate Thunderclap Newman's call to arms.

Pity poor George Markstein! I expect he enjoyed *It's Your Funeral*, a solid, well done, parapolitics-themed thriller. He was still trying to track down writers to contribute to a series about a rebel secret agent in a mind-control debriefing camp; while coming into increasing conflict with a partner/actor/writer/director who had begun to see their shared project in singularly different terms...

9

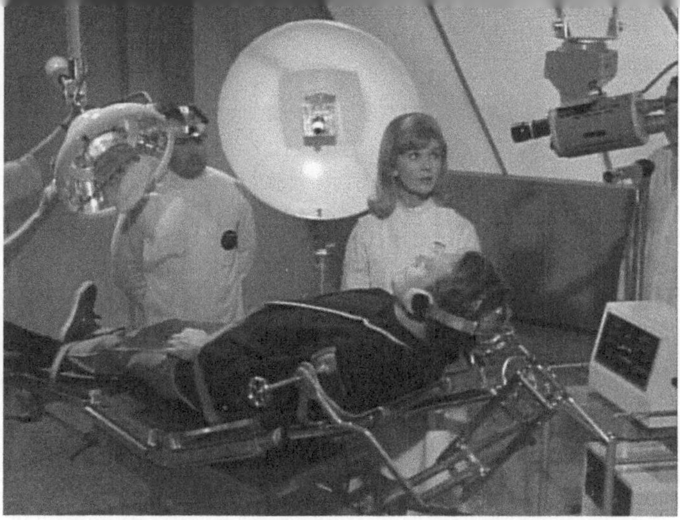

Episode Nine

A CHANGE OF MIND

In February 1967, Lew Grade screened the print of *Arrival* for a team of CBS executives, and McGoohan went to meet them at their office in London. Their chief outlined his concerns about a series in which the hero remained a prisoner. American audiences, he warned, might view such a person as a 'loser'. McGoohan politely declined to follow his advice, and left. When the exec asked Grade how he managed to get along with this individual, Grade replied, 'I always give in to what he wants.'

Back at MGM Studios, having sacked the director of *It's Your Funeral*, McGoohan fired the next show's director, Roy Rossotti, and directed it himself, using the pseudonym of 'Joseph Serf'. The screenwriter was Roger Parkes.

A Change of Mind is the third episode in which Number 6 emerges victorious. We find him exercising in the woods, where he has built a gymnasium, including bars and a punch bag, out of forest products. He is accosted by a couple of thugs, and gives them a sound beating. Fleeing, they threaten to report his aggressive tendencies to 'the Committee'.

In the Council Chambers, Number 6 witnesses a pathetic self-criticism session and intimidates the Citizens Welfare Committee, who wear top hats and striped, burglar sweatshirts. He is accused of having 'a spirit of social disharmony'. The Committee breaks for tea and a medical report. The New Number 2 (John Sharpe) warns him that this is serious stuff, and introduces him to Number 86 (Angela Browne), who was once disharmonious herself, and who invites him to attend a Social Progress Group meeting. This too goes badly. Number 6's ironic demeanour gets him called a reactionary, a rebel, and disharmonious. He is taken to The Hospital for his medical. In the Aversion Therapy corridor, he witnesses a man being terrified by film of Rover and the word 'Unmutual'.

In the corridor, Number 6 meets two patients with scars on their temples. In the screenplay, they are called LOBO MEN. One of them explains that he was Unmutual, before the lobotomy. Now the Citizens Welfare Committee declares Number 6 Unmutual. Its chairman warns him, 'should any further complaint be lodged against you, it will be necessary to propose you for the treatment known as Instant Social Conversion.' In the street, Number 6 is shunned. Loudspeaker announcements warn the Villagers that 'Number 6 has been declared Unmutual until further notice. Any unsocial incident involving Number 6 should be reported immediately to the Appeals Sub-Committee.'

At home, he is visited by the Appeals Sub-Committee, a group of matrons who insist he must conform or face loneliness and an enforced lobotomy. Number 2 claims he is powerless to intervene and help him.

NUMBER 2: 'A scapegoat? Is that what you think? ... You'll soon have lasting peace of mind and adjustment to the social system here ... Isolation of the aggressive frontal lobes of the brain.'

Interested villagers are invited to visit The Hospital and watch Number 6's lobotomy live on closed-circuit TV. He is mobbed, beaten by the Sub-Committee's umbrellas, and dragged to The Hospital, where he is shot up with drugs.

Strapped to a table, Number 6 witnesses what appear to be the preparations for an 'ultrasonic lobotomy' – performed by none other than Number 86, his former ally. Again, the repetition of meaningless words and numbers creates high drama as she focuses the ultrasonic beam.

NUMBER 86: 'Three centimetres in.
One point five centimetres up...
Point four-five centimetres right.
Point zero-two-three centimetres down.
Point zero-zero-one-five up.
Hold the horizontal. Precise!'

Shot up with more drugs, The Prisoner passes out. When he wakes he is told the operation has been a success – but he is being tricked. The 'muscle relaxants' he has been receiving are mind-control drugs. Number 86 is taxed to keep Number 6 stupefied by lacing his tea with eight-grain doses of 'Mytol'. Number 6 avoids drinking the tea.

That night he is awoken by Number 2, keen to know why he resigned. The scene is played in a tight two-shot, almost as close as the shots of McGoohan and McKern in *Once Upon A Time.*

This is most effective. Number 6 is able to convince Number 2 that he believes his aggressive tendencies have been curtailed, and that he can't quite remember the answer to Number 2's question. But when the thugs return to his backwoods gym, Number 6 is able to beat the bejesus out of them again. He realises he has been drugged, not brain-damaged. Back home, he switches teacups and gets Number 86 completely high on Mytol.

NUMBER 86: 'I want to make him happy...'

NUMBER 6: 'The ecstasy of illusion.'

NUMBER 86: 'I'm high. I'm high as Number 2...'

Number 6 hypnotises Number 86 and sets out to turn the tables on Number 2. He insists he wants to reveal why he resigned, and also to encourage the other Villagers to reveal their secrets. Number 2 readily agrees that Number 6 may make a public confession in The Village Square. But before he can reveal all, Number 86 denounces Number 2 as an Unmutual. Number 6 bombards the crowd with the same message – adding, 'You can still salvage your rights as individuals. Your rights to truth and free thought!' by following his orders. The mob turns on Number 2, who is forced to flee.

Though still a prisoner, Number 6 has achieved another victory.

WHAT HAVE WE LEARNED?

The self-criticism and jargon recall Soviet-style prison or labour camps, and suggest that the Russians could be running the show. But the way the Villagers enthusiastically embrace the scapegoating of Number 6 and his apparent lobotomy suggests that these tendencies may be universal, rather than regime-specific. Imprisonment in psychiatric hospitals was practised in both East and West; lobotomy was a popular treatment among insane doctors and callous family members throughout the Western world. Eighty per cent of American lobotomies were apparently performed on women. Joseph Kennedy, millionaire father of JFK, insisted that his oldest daughter, Rosemary, receive one. The ghastly operation wrecked her mind, leaving her with limited motor and speaking skills.

While ending on a high note for The Prisoner, this is the most pessimistic episode so far. Apart from the mob scene at the end of *Dance of the Dead*, the Villagers have generally been compliant and docile. In *A Change of Mind* they are enthusiastically complicit in their indoctrination, eager to turn violent and sadistic on anyone they or the authorities choose to scapegoat. The watchmaker's dissident faction has vanished, if it ever existed. The only rebel spirit who remains is Number 6, issuing orders for people to think for themselves.

10

Episode Ten

THE GENERAL

The General was written by Lewis Greifer, under the pen name of 'Joshua Adam'. The director was Peter Graham Scott, who had directed half a dozen episodes of *Danger Man*. Scott, under contract to the BBC, received word one Friday that McGoohan had fired yet another director, Robert Lynn, and needed a replacement to start shooting on Monday. Scott assumed this would be impossible but someone – either producer Tomblin or executive producer McGoohan – was able to arrange a leave of absence for him to direct *The General*.

In *The Schizoid Man* we learned that you cannot take a meeting with the General. Thanks perhaps to the persistence of Markstein as story editor, a brief aside in one episode now becomes the central puzzle of another.

Number 6 is having a coffee at the outdoor cafe when a male voice on the speaker system directs all students to their televisions, as the next instalment of the Professor's Three Part History Course is about to be broadcast by the General's Department. Everyone leaves save Number 6 and a young man, Number 12 (John Castle). Even their waiter is shutting up shop so that he can take the televised course. 'Best of luck with your exams' has replaced 'Be seeing you' as The Village catchphrase. Number 12 suggests that Number 6 give the Professor's course (advertised in posters as '100% entry, 100% pass') a try. Sirens are heard and Number 12 observes that the Professor (Peter Howell) is running away, pursued by a mob.

Collapsing on the beach, the Professor is carried back to The Village. Number 6 finds a tape recorder, apparently dropped by same, and conceals it in the sand. He watches the Professor's lecture on TV in his cottage. It is preceded by an intense 'sales pitch', in which an Announcer insists that the Professor's work has:

> 'a significance far beyond the confines of this community. To quote our friend, the Professor, Speedlearn is nothing less than a revolution in Educational Technique. The latest figure shows a 72.4% enrollment on the Three Years in Three Minutes History Course. Many thanks and congratulations. And I think we can promise the General that we will improve even on that figure.'

None the worse for his escape attempt, the Professor starts his lecture with another pitch for Speedlearn:

> 'It is quite simply the most important, the most far reaching, most beneficent development in mass education since the beginning of time. A marriage of Science and Mass Communication which results in the abolition of years of tedious and wasteful schooling.

> 'A three years' course indelibly impressed on the mind in three minutes! Impossible! That's what I said until I was introduced to the General. And then I realised that not only was it possible, but that education was ready to take a giant leap forward from the Dark Ages into the Twentieth and Twenty-first centuries...'

Number 6 watches the 15-second 'lecture' and then discovers that he possesses a lot of useless information which he didn't know before – including facts and dates from the Napoleonic Wars. A new, milk-drinking, Number 2 (Colin Gordon) comes visiting, accompanied by a young man with a detecting device. They are looking for the Professor's tape recorder. Number 2 suggests that Number 6 might be released if he turns over the recorder. Number 6 distrusts the offer, and they fall into a rote-repetition of facts from the Professor's latest lecture, which Number 2 insists is 'a great experiment. You can learn a lot!'

That night, Number 6 returns to the beach. But Number 12 has beaten him there, and found the tape recorder. Claiming to be on his side, he gives Number 6 the machine, which he calls 'your passport out of here'. Number 6 plays the tape which features the Professor's denunciation of Speedlearn and the General:

> 'You are being tricked. Speedlearn is an abomination. It is slavery. If you want to be free, there is only one way. Destroy the General! ... The General must be destroyed!'

Back at the Dome, Number 2 and Number 12 discuss the Professor and his eccentricities. Number 12, playing both sides, suggests a harder line be taken. Meanwhile the Professor is pumped for further lecture material by white-coated 'therapists'. At the Town Hall, Number 6 and the Town Councillors, clad in top hats and funeral attire, gather beneath the eye-in-the-pyramid chair and a huge, black, Penny Farthing logo. And Number 6 joins an art-as-therapy class run by the Professor's wife (Betty McDowall). She shows him examples of what she claims is good student work: a young man tearing pages out of a book.

MME. PROFESSOR 'He's creating a fresh concept: "Construction arises from the ashes of destruction." And that woman – '

NUMBER 6 'Standing on her head?'

MME. PROFESSOR 'She's developing a new perspective.'

Number 6 shows her a colour sketch he has made – a portrait of Mme. Professor in a general's uniform. She is not amused, and tears the picture in two. That evening he sneaks into their mansion, where Mme. Professor confronts him among her busts of prominent Villagers – including various Number 2s, and Number 6 himself. She insists that she and her husband are not prisoners, but here as volunteers. Number 2 appears and tells Number 6 it won't be possible for him to see the Professor – he indicates, in an adjacent room, the form of the sleeping savant. Number 6 enters with a walking stick and smashes the head of a wax dummy, created by Mme. Professor to resemble her husband – who is underground, working non-stop in the service of Speedlearn. Number 2 says the offer of freedom has been rescinded. Number 6 hands over the tape recorder in any case.

On the streets, The Prisoner encounters a student 'demonstration' – frolickers rejoicing and carrying placards and banners celebrating Speedlearn. Greifer's script makes an interesting choice: 'A fair proportion are long haired and bearded.' But the chance to associate mind-controlled Villagers with the nascent Hippie movement wasn't pursued: the MGM studio extras are the usual, clean-cut crew.

Back at his cottage, one of the lamps short-circuits, and Number 6 is immediately visited by an electrician and an administrator – Number 12. Number 12 says that while the power is out they can talk freely, and asks Number 6 if he'd like to get the Professor's anti-Speedlearn message out. Number 6 says he would. Number 12 gives him a pen which contains a miniaturised recording of the Professor's speech. The next day, while Number 12 addresses the Council Chamber about Speedlearn, Number 6 overpowers two guards and gets access to the information-network 'projection room' from which the next lecture will be broadcast. He replaces the lecture file with the Professor's denunciation – but Number 2 spots him on a surveillance screen, and sends more guards to knock him out and insert the correct lecture, moments before it is broadcast.

Number 6 is interrogated by Number 12 and Number 2. Number 2 insists that Number 6 has received assistance and that there must be a rebel cell in The Village. He tells Mme. Professor he must keep her husband working until the current lecture series is complete. Then he decides to seek the General's assistance. In the tunnels beneath The Village, Number 6 is introduced to the genius behind Speedlearn, the General: a large computer with a lab-coated attendant.

NUMBER 2: 'This mess of circuits, my dear chap, is as revolutionary as nuclear fission. No more wastage in schools. No tedious rote learning. A brilliantly-devised course, delivered by a leading teacher, subliminally learned and checked and corrected by an infallible authority... and what do we have?

NUMBER 6: 'A row of cabbages.'

NUMBER 2: 'Indeed. Knowledgeable cabbages.'

NUMBER 6: 'But what kind of knowledge?'

NUMBER 2: 'For the time being past history will do. Shortly we'll be making our own.'

Number 2 intends to ask the General who Number 6's collaborator is. Knowing that this will expose Number 12, Number 6 proposes to ask 'a question that can't be answered' first. He types one word, which is punch-card-ised and fed to the General. It causes the General to overheat and short-circuit. The Professor attempts to switch his creation off and is electrocuted. Rushing to save the Professor, Number 12 is electrocuted, too.

Aghast and defeated, Number 2 asks what The Prisoner did. Number 6 tells him he asked the simple question, 'Why?'.

(Usually an episode would end at this point, with bars closing across The Prisoner's face. But in the script and the finished show there is a final, single-shot scene, reminiscent of the last moments of *The Third Man*, in which Mme. Professor waits for news of her husband, and Number 6, walking away from camera, passes her, and – presumably – tells her that he is dead. It's an elegant coda.)

WHAT HAVE WE LEARNED?

First and foremost, this is another episode in which The Village is kidnapping scientists (Mme. Professor claims they volunteered to be here, but it is obvious neither can leave) and putting them to work. It's becoming clear, viewing the episodes in their production order, that Number 6 has more in common with these scientists than he does with John Drake, Secret Agent. We shall return to this shortly.

In *The General*, The Village is the site of an experiment in 'speed learning'. Almost three-quarters of the Villagers – including administrators like Number 2 and Number 12 – have enrolled in the Professor's course. For now the technique is being tried on a closed community, but as the Announcer says, it's expected that Speedlearn will have a much wider roll-out. Soon it's apparent that Speedlearn is another form of mind control: one which embeds rote-learned information in the brain. Snippets of knowledge are not the same as wisdom, but as far as Number 2 is concerned they're all that's necessary for a severely-surveilled, servile population to be reliably ordered.

In the West today, Speedlearn might be enthusiastically espoused by many educational 'reformers'. An attractive project for any capitalist, rote-learned information, repeated parrot-fashion, would also have been an appealing prospect for the Communist bloc. The use of The Village as a petri dish for Speedlearn suggests that what McKern's Number 2 said was right, and that the interests of both Cold War adversaries have become identical. The Professor might have developed Speedlearn at MIT and Oxford, or it and he could equally be products of Soviet educational and computer science.

If Number 2 is being truthful when he offers Number 6 his freedom, the General and Speedlearn are of paramount importance to the controllers of The Village. Even if he's lying, he clearly prioritises Speedlearn over any working relationship with Number 6. So The Village is involved in more than just interrogation and mind control: it's a generator of intellectual property, of a potentially enormous value-stream. By wrecking the General, Number 6 has, at least for now, foiled the roll-out of Speedlearn. This is his fourth victorious episode in a row. But surely victory comes at a cost. The Professor and Number 12 are dead, incalculable revenue has been lost, and we can reasonably anticipate problems for The Prisoner in the next episode.

Attempts to replicate Villagers such as Number 6 or the Electrician/Gardener pair appear to have ended. As a figurehead for Speedlearn, surely a clone of the Professor would have been more useful than a wax dummy!

The Undertakers are out in force in this episode, and we see Number 2 dressed in funeral garb for the first time. A new costume element appears, also: the military-style guards who protect the inner reaches of the Town Hall. The script describes them thus: 'Smart and tough. They are neatly attired in one-piece, overall uniforms. White boxing boots, white gauntlet gloves. Deep white belts. Green visor caps and sunglasses. They carry white truncheons with hand straps.' In production, the green visor caps were replaced with white helmets: the uniform overall looks like a cross between NATO and American military police. It will reappear. Is the implication that Village policing is being done by the military now – as opposed to being left to stripey-shirted thugs and Rover? Or are we encountering a separate level of security, one which guards much deeper secrets in the caves beneath The Village?

And why has a male voice replaced Fielding's on The Village PA system?

11

Episode Eleven

A. B. AND C.

A. B. and C. was written by Anthony Skene, and directed by Pat Jackson. It was shot at MGM immediately after *The General*. It's the weakest of all the episodes. Tomblin had told Skene to write a script using as much Portmeirion stock footage as possible. Disliking the assignment, Skene took a walk around the backlot at MGM, and came up with a story to be shot on the 'French' locations there, instead. *A. B. and C.* relies on several replays of the opening credits sequence – to remind us that Number 6 has resigned. Number 6 spends much of the episode asleep and dreaming.

This is the second show to feature Colin Gordon as Number 2. Though it was broadcast before *The General*, it's clearly meant to follow that episode. Number 2 has lost his former confidence and is terrified of his superiors following the collapse of Speedlearn. He stammers into the telephone, 'I *am* doing my best… I know I'm not indispensable.' Number 2's milk consumption has risen (in the script he has numerous milk bottles lined up ready to go; in the episode, the Butler serves him his milk in glasses) so presumably his ulcer is getting worse. Number 2 seems heavily dependent on a new lab-coated scientist, Number 14 (Sheila Allen). Number 14 is developing an experimental drug which influences the subject's dreams while the experimenters watch those dreams unfold on the big screen. Number 2 is convinced that Number 6 resigned in order to offer his services to another party, and has three suspects – whom he calls A, B and C.

Number 14 warns him that three doses of the drug – which has not yet been tested on animals – are all a person can take: a fourth will kill them. Number 2 insists the risk is worth it. Number 14 has Number 6 transported, unconscious, to her underground laboratory, gives him his first dose, and plugs him into dream cassette A, which activates a dream of one of 'Mme. Engadine's celebrated parties', in Paris, where he will meet Suspect A. Mme. Engadine's residence looks a great deal like that of the Professor and his wife in *The General* – but this is a dream, so no matter. At the party, Number 6 – elegantly clad in black tie and tuxedo, *à la* Bond – tells Mme. Engadine (Katherine Kath) that he is planning to take a holiday. He quickly encounters the dashingly moustachioed A (Peter Bowles), a defector who 'made world news a few years ago'.

A and a couple of henchmen attempt to kidnap Number 6 in a Citroen. But, taking control of his dream, he is able to defeat all three of them with some well-placed knockout blows. Number 2 wants to try a second dream immediately, but Number 14 insists it is too dangerous, and that they must wait a day before continuing the experiment.

The next morning, Number 6 encounters Number 14 in The Village cafe, and remembers her from his dream. He confronts Number 2, and shows him the scar from the drug injection on his wrist. Number 2 feigns ignorance, but after Number 6 has gone he promises his telephonic masters that within two days they will know why Number 6 resigned. 'You have my word… I realise my future's at stake. Two days: I guarantee.' That evening, a Maid enters Number 6's residence with an evening nightcap. (In the script, she speaks an unintelligible Arabic. In the filmed version, she does not speak at all.) Surprisingly compliant, The Prisoner drinks it, and collapses unconscious on the floor. In her underground lab, Number 14 inserts dream cassette B. She and Number 2 monitor his progress as he returns to Mme. Engadine's Parisian *salon*.

Number 6 meets B (Annette Carell) in a bower in Engadine's garden. They exchange pleasantries and dance. Concerned that the dream is going nowhere, Number 2 insists they change the dream in order to put B's life in jeopardy. For the first time in the series, a gun appears – pointed by a threatening bruiser at B's head. B begs The Prisoner to reveal why he resigned, or she will be killed. But Number 6 reuses Number 2's ruse from *The Schizoid Man* – peppering B with questions only the real B could answer: how long has her husband been dead? How old is her son? What is his name? B's folders don't contain sufficient information, and, when she cannot answer, Number 6 abandons her to her dream-fate.

Waking, Number 6 finds another injection scar on his wrist. He follows Number 14 into the woods and discovers the entrance to her underground laboratory. With ease, he sneaks into the lab via a ventilation shaft, and watches an on-screen playback of one of his dreams. Understanding the game, he empties her third syringe and fills it with water from a glass.

That night he doesn't drink his sleeping draught, and plays unconscious. Number 14 injects him, unknowingly, with water. Absent the drugs, Number 6 is able to control his dream.

While her guests dance a conga line, Mme. Engadine and Number 6 produce two keys and open a double-locked door. They leave the party and she drives him through a rear-screen projection of the Champs-Elysées at night. Their journey ends at the church set on the MGM backlot. Number 2 and Number 14 conclude that Engadine is C, whose identity they have not previously known. But C is merely a conduit to D, a masked character waiting on the far side of the church door. Number 6 unmasks D, who is revealed to be Number 2. He hands over an envelope which Number 2 hopes will contain the secret of his resignation. But it merely holds brochures – for holidays in Italy and Greece.

Even in his sleep, Number 6 has won again. Number 2 looks up in terror as a curved, red phone – the hotline to his superiors – rings.

WHAT HAVE WE LEARNED?

Not a great deal. Since these are dreams, presumably the information contained within them is about as reliable as any dream information. In his first dream, Number 6 meets A, a defector with whom he used to work.

A: 'We both do the same jobs.'

NUMBER 6: 'For different reasons.'

A: 'I see you overrate "absolute truth". Whichever way you look at it, we both want to conquer the world.'

What profession conquers the world? The spy's? Hardly. Spies – even when they become President of the United States or Russia – are mere adjuncts to a large and vastly more powerful military-industrial-corporate complex. They work to promote the interests of their masters; they do not 'conquer the world'. In the script, Number 6 calls B 'the most glamorous spy in the business'. In the episode, he says she was 'the most intriguing spy I ever met' – but neither suggests that their profession was the same. Apart from the tuxedo, I see no evidence here that Number 6 was an espionage agent, even in his dreams. The focus of this episode is, as in *The General*, on the diabolical misuse of science. Number 2 encourages Number 14 to pursue her dangerous experiment with the words, 'Where is your scientific enthusiasm?'

So, at the end of this unreliable episode, we know that Number 6 has friends in Paris (hardly surprising: he's a well-to-do Londoner with a taste for travel), that he's able to slip into a building via an easily-accessible ventilator – hardly a masterpiece of spycraft – and that he can take control of matters when he has unpleasant dreams, a useful skill indeed. No light is shed on his profession. But the nature and purpose of The Village are becoming increasingly clear.

12

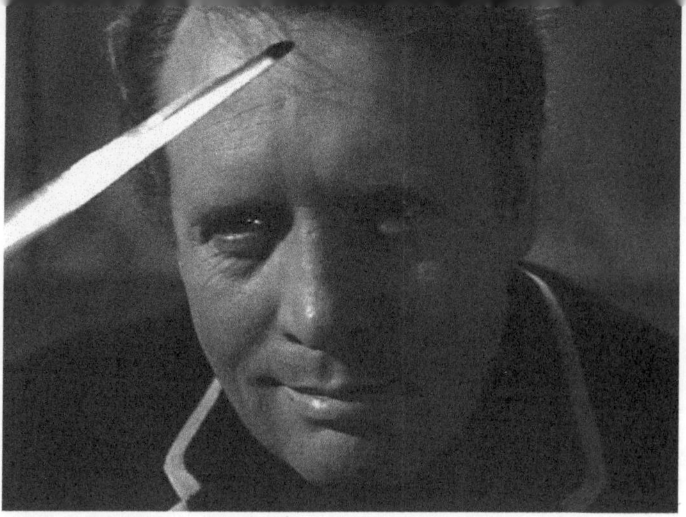

Episode Twelve
HAMMER INTO ANVIL

This episode, too, was directed by Pat Jackson. The writer was Roger Woddis. Woddis, who died in 1993, has only four television credits. If Markstein chose him to write an episode, he showed surprising taste: Woddis was a poet, a humourist, and a committed left-winger, whose anti-Thatcher poetry from the 1980s is quite splendid. Perhaps thanks to the author's politics, the episode provides Number 6 with a moral purpose beyond mere escape: revenge. *Hammer into Anvil* relies on a fair amount of Portmeirion footage: the first episode to do so since *Dance of the Dead*. A second-unit crew had visited Portmeirion in March 1967, with Maher doubling McGoohan: the Maher footage is readily identifiable since it consists either of long shots or of shots of the back of his head. But a couple of sequences feature McGoohan himself, alone on one of his weekend visits.

The New Number 2 (Patrick Cargill) is a sadistic individual with a propensity for violence. We first encounter him in The Hospital, interrogating Number 73 (Hilary Dwyer), who has attempted suicide. She has been brought to The Village because its owners are trying to locate her husband, a person of some significance who has gone missing. Number 2 produces an incriminating photograph in an attempt to coerce her. From outside the building, her screams are heard. Number 6, who happens to be nearby, hears the cries and rushes into The Hospital. Restrained by thugs in white lab coats, he is too late to help. Number 73 is dead, having jumped – or been pushed – out of the window. Infuriated, Number 2 turns on Number 6. Number 6 insists that Number 2 will pay for this, and leaves.

When Number 6 refuses to respond to his summons to the Dome, Number 2 sends four thugs to bring him. In previous episodes, various Number 2s have carried a 'shooting stick' – a combination umbrella/fold-out seat popular among the British horse-racing set. Number 2's shooting stick is now revealed to contain a sword, with which he threatens The Prisoner. When Number 6 refuses to be intimidated, Number 2 slaps him across the face, and addresses him in German:

NUMBER 2: 'Du musst Amboss oder Hammer sein.'

NUMBER 6: 'You must be anvil or hammer.'

NUMBER 2: 'I see you know your Goethe.'

Number 2 considers himself the hammer, and The Prisoner his anvil. Number 6 is clear on the concept, and believes the opposite. After a call from the red phone shows that Number 2 is timorous before his superiors (as bullies generally are), Number 6 begins a campaign of actions to bring his adversary down. His first stop is The Village shop, where he listens to five identical records of Bizet's *L'Arlésiene*. This induces the shop assistant to report him to Number 2, who listens to them all but can discern no difference between them. He is more disturbed by the copy of the *Tally Ho!* the shop assistant hands him: beneath the headline 'Increase Vigilance Call by Number 2', Number 6 has circled the word 'security' and added a question mark. Number 2 and his assistant Number 14 (Basil Hoskins) watch as the surveillance cameras in Number 6's cottage show him penning a note. Number 14 goes to the cottage and retrieves the underlying piece of paper. Not surprisingly, Number 6 has left a clearly-etched copy of his message for Number 14 to find: 'Number 2's instability confirmed. Detailed report follows. D.6.'

Number 2 immediately falls for the ruse, and assumes Number 6 is a 'plant', placed in The Village to spy on him. This is quite a striking turn of events: it suggests that Number 6 has become so embedded in The Village hierarchy that he is able to intimidate his interrogators with ease. But perhaps it isn't surprising. He has been here for a while, and knows The Village systems as well as any prisoner can. Number 2, despite his violence and intimidating manner, is a total newcomer. That night Number 2 and Number 14 follow Number 6 to the 'stone boat', where Number 6 has concealed an envelope full of papers. Distrustful even of his assistant, Number 2 dismisses Number 14 and sends the pages to Number 243 (Michael Segal) in the Laboratory. To Number 2's alarm, Number 243 reports that the pages are all blank. Seething with paranoia, Number 2 accuses Number 243 of being 'in with him'.

Next day, Number 6 places a quote from Cervantes, in Spanish, in the *Tally Ho!* personal ads: 'Hay mas mal en el aldea que se suena' ('there is more evil in the village than you can dream of'). Then he telephones Number 249 (Norman Scace) – the director of psychiatrics at The Hospital – and requests a report on Number 2. The director reports this to Number 2, who listens to the recording of their conversation and uses high-tech oscilloscope patterns to identify the voice of Number 6. He demands to know why The Prisoner called The Hospital with this enquiry. The director of psychiatry says he doesn't know, and Number 2 explodes.

NUMBER 2: 'He had a reason for phoning you. What was it?'

DIRECTOR: 'Why don't you ask him?'

NUMBER 2: 'Would you like to sit in this chair?'

DIRECTOR: 'I was merely suggesting –'

NUMBER 2: 'Don't you tell me what to do! You can go.'

DIRECTOR: 'Thank you.'

This is a splendidly English exchange: behind the director's frosty politeness, it is clear another enemy has been made. It's apparent that The Prisoner – once a pawn, in *Checkmate* – now seems able to 'PWN' the entire place, at least when his adversary is as unstable as this Number 2.

Number 6 continues his campaign. He requests the Bizet song from the orchestra in the bandstand, and walks away. The bandmaster reports this to Number 2, who abuses him and makes another enemy. In the Control Room, the Supervisor (played again by Peter Swanwick) is doing double-duty as The Village's DJ, playing record requests over the radio network. He reads a message from Number 113 to Number 6, dedicating a song to him 'on his birthday'. This sends Number 2 into a fury, because Number 113 is dead, and it isn't Number 6's birthday. He and Number 14 race to the Control Room, where he asks the mystified Supervisor what the message means. When the Supervisor remarks that 'It means what it says', Number 2 relieves him of his post. Raging at all the technicians there, Number 2 vows to 'break this conspiracy!'

Worried about Number 2's mental state, Number 14 proposes the murder of The Prisoner. He warns his boss that Number 6 is 'out to poison the entire Village'. But Number 2 just rails at the unfortunate Butler and is entirely intimidated when Number 6 shows up, claiming that Number 2 has invited him to an urgent meeting. Infuriated, Number 14 challenges Number 6 to a bout of Koshu in the Recreation Hall.

This second bout of Koshu is thankfully brief. The game ends inconclusively when other contestants appear, and Number 6 returns to The Village shop, where he buys a cuckoo clock. This he leaves on Number 2's doorstep, keeping only the box the clock came in. While Number 2, in a panic, calls the bomb squad, Number 6 uses the box to catch a pigeon. He releases the bird, which the Control Room tracks and captures. Sure enough, it bears a message apparently in code: '20, 60, 40, 47, 76' and so forth.

The Village computer – one assumes a lower-specced successor to the General – produces a translation, indicating that a vital message will be sent tomorrow. Sure enough, Number 6 signals in Morse Code from the beach – but the Control Room cannot locate a recipient, and, as in *Once Upon A Time*, his only intelligible message is a nursery rhyme. This time, not even the computer can assist: it simply reprints the input. Garbage in, garbage out. Number 2 is distraught. Meanwhile, in the cafe, Number 6 borrows Number 14's menu, knowing that the waiter will report their 'meeting' to higher authority.

Back at the Dome, Number 2 accuses Number 14 of being a traitor and throws him out. In a paranoid frenzy, he fires the Butler, too. Number 14 is quite distraught and goes to Number 6's cottage to confront him. They fight, to the tune of Vivaldi's *Four Seasons*, causing considerable destruction. Having knocked Number 14 out, Number 6 returns to the Dome. Number 2, a shadow of his former self, accuses him of being a plant, sent by their masters to spy on him. Number 6 rightly observes that if this is so, then Number 2 should have had nothing to fear. Surveillance in The Village is simply business as usual. Instead, by confronting Number 6 and attempting to thwart his monitoring, he has committed 'sabotage'. (Village *aficionados* might prefer that Number 2 be declared Unmutual. But this opportunity for story continuity was missed.)

Number 6 instructs Number 2 to call his bosses and report himself as in need of replacement. Number 2, a broken man, picks up the red phone and does exactly that. While still a prisoner, Number 6 is now the most powerful individual in The Village. He has triumphed once again.

WHAT HAVE WE LEARNED?

In the 1960s, British spies and business visitors to Russia were often warned that the Russians would attempt to get them in compromising sexual situations and take photographs of them. So Number 2's use of the blackmail photo may suggest Russian tradecraft.

But all authoritarian governments – as we know to our cost – are paranoid and constantly on the lookout for conspiracies. Richard Nixon was now President of the United States; within a decade, Harold Wilson in England, Gough Whitlam in Australia, and Willy Brandt, in West Germany would all lose power to what were often seen as conspiracies mounted by their own intelligence agencies. A conspiracy, after all, is no more than an agreement by two or more persons to commit a crime, and those who accuse others of being 'conspiracy buffs' are often world-class conspirators themselves. Number 6's strategy of destabilising a paranoid regime would work no matter which side runs The Village.

The apparent 'bomb plot' references contemporary events. The 1960s and 1970s saw a series of bomb explosions, set by the IRA, to undercut support for English control of Northern Ireland. We all grew up with the possibility of bombs, and with bomb threats, but we got on with our lives regardless: the media-stoked paranoia, imprisonment without trial, and armed troop deployments which we know today would have been unthinkable in England in 1967. Woddis' script depicts Number 2's paranoid response to the cuckoo clock, and its deconstruction in a sandbagged, bomb disposal area, as ludicrous overreactions. So, again, the implication may be that Number 2 is working not for Her Majesty's Government, but for some more excitable, foreign regime.

Number 6's sending a coded message via passenger pigeon might suggest that he has intel skills, and undercut my developing theory that he is not a spy. He appears to have sent a message in numeric code – but has he? Surely the point of *Hammer into Anvil* is that The Prisoner isn't relying on any real spy tradecraft, but is simply posting ambiguous, contradictory messages, in order to mess with Number 2's mind. We've already seen him destroy one computer, simply by asking it the question 'Why?' Could he not, here, be doing something similar – providing meaningless numbers to the next-gen computer, confident that it will attempt to make 'sense' out of them, even when there is no sense to be made? Just as, today, intel agencies known by their acronyms trawl our emails and our telephone conversations and our internet searches, and then leak evidence of conspiracies ('X just happened; our intelligence was powerless to prevent this but discovered the whole story later') where quite different conspiracies may actually exist. Garbage in, garbage out.

So I want to suggest what seems likely to me: that Number 6 in *Hammer into Anvil* is faking spy tradecraft, about which he knows little, so as to disturb Number 2. On the other hand, if you – like George Markstein – are a firm believer that The Prisoner was John Drake, then this excellent episode contains the strongest (indeed perhaps the only) evidence for this so far.

The fact that The Prisoner knows Morse Code certainly doesn't make him a spy. Per *Once Upon A Time*, if he had been an RAF aviator or bombardier he would be proficient in this simple code. In the 1960s, anyone who was a member of the Wolf Cubs or the Brownies was familiar with Morse, too, if only to send an SOS message.

13

Episode Thirteen
MANY HAPPY RETURNS

The last episode of the first series was shot in October 1967. The script was by Anthony Skene, author of *Dance of the Dead* and *A. B. and C.*, and the director was to be Michael Truman. Truman began the shoot, but either fell ill or fell foul of the leading actor, and departed after a few days. McGoohan directed the rest, using his previous pseudonym of 'Joseph Serf'. This choice of pseudonym is interesting, and perhaps enlightening. Actors and musicians who become popular or financially viable are subject to a considerable amount of manipulation by their financiers and rights-holders. Sooner or later, some of them resent this. The resulting mindset can lead wealthy TV, film and rock stars – who in reality have a fair degree of autonomy – to view themselves as victims.

Having made this mistake, some of them fall into a pattern of self-pity – sometimes servile self-pity – where they abandon certain commitments, embark on others, and romanticise their imagined servitude.

By the end of 1967, Patrick McGoohan may have been exhibiting these tendencies – a horrible form of mind control in their own right. McGoohan was, reportedly, the best-paid actor in British television. He was the star/producer/writer/director of his own dramatic series – an immensely demanding job which involved an expensive, complex, high-quality 35mm TV series no one had, as yet, seen. Under considerable pressure, McGoohan had fought with fellow actors, encountered difficulties with his business partners, and fired various directors whom he should never have hired. What was he to do at this stage? I can think of three clear options: 1) Take total control of the series, write and direct the whole show for as long as it lasted, no matter what the physical and emotional cost; 2) act resentful, claim to be ill-used as *The Prisoner*'s 'serf', and flee to Hollywood for validation; or 3) rebuild bridges with Grade and Markstein and get ITC to commit to a 13-episode second season, staying involved throughout so as to ensure the same level of storytelling quality (by which I mean that I think Markstein and McGoohan were equally interested in story content, and Grade was clearly their champion in terms of story delivery).

McGoohan made choice number 2, the worst choice, and validation quickly came, in the form of a three-picture deal with MGM. His first assignment was a supporting role in a Hollywood blockbuster called *Ice Station Zebra*. The shoot would be in Los Angeles, and he would have to be gone for weeks at a time, during production of the second season of *The Prisoner*. For Lew Grade, McGoohan's decision to take off must have been a clear sign that the actor whom he most admired was cooling on their project. For Markstein, Meyer, Tomblin, Tobias-Shaw and the rest of the crew, *Ice Station Zebra* might be taken as notice that their days on this project were numbered. For McGoohan, who knows what it meant? The man was no fool, but nor would he be the first actor seduced by the siren songs of Hollywood.

The choice of the name Joseph 'Serf' (one of the characters in Hermann Hesse's novel *The Glass Bead Game*) still seems excessive. McGoohan was no one's serf. He'd been given something close to carte blanche to produce and direct an entirely original British TV series with feature-film budgets. Nothing like this had ever occurred before (nor would it happen again). As an alternative to *Once Upon A Time*, *Many Happy Returns* concludes the first season very well, though it suffers a hiccup in the casting area. It also provides the definitive answer as to who runs The Village, as we shall see.

Number 6 awakes in his cottage to find no water in the taps, no muzak coming from the radio, and no phone signal. Outside, The Village appears to have been abandoned. The shop is closed, the cafe tables overturned. Number 2's Dome is deserted too. The departure of the Butler in *Hammer into Anvil* has been followed, it appears, by everybody else. Only the black cat remains. (In the screenplay, Number 6 visits The Hospital and releases the lab rats, a noble gesture, and tries unsuccessfully to get the helicopter running. Neither is essential to the narrative.)

In the forest, The Prisoner fells another tree and builds a raft. He breaks into the shop and leaves an IOU for provisions and a camera. He signs it 'No. 6?' He studiously photographs the buildings of The Village, puts the film in a plastic bag, and sets sail. He creates a compass with a needle, magnetised by his

Village radio speaker. He is at sea for 25 days, heading slowly, it appears, on a north-east course. (This sequence, largely without music, is most effective.) Then he runs afoul of gun runners, who steal his belongings and throw him overboard. Boarding their boat, he overpowers them and steers for land. When the criminals break free, he jumps ship and swims for the shore.

He wakes on a beach adjacent to a lighthouse. He climbs white cliffs, and follows a silent man to his camp, where a gypsy woman gives him food and directs him to a road. (In the screenplay the gypsy girl is a cockney who tells him they are in Kent. But this joke is not used.) Number 6 sees a British police constable directing traffic. He avoids a roadblock – which he automatically assumes is looking for him – and jumps aboard an open cargo truck. He falls asleep. Waking suddenly, he hears sirens and makes a flying leap from the back of the truck.

He finds himself in central London, adjacent to Marble Arch.

This is no fake, as it was in *The Chimes of Big Ben*. It is the city that he used to live in. Unshaven, penniless and ragged, he walks to 1 Buckingham Place. He hesitates before knocking. A stern maid opens the front door.

MAID: 'Yes?'

NUMBER 6: 'Who owns this house?'

MAID: 'I beg your pardon?'

NUMBER 6: 'I'm sorry, what I meant to say was, I'd like to see your master.'

MAID: 'My mistress is not at home.'

The maid closes the door. How quaint! This was another time, indeed. And The Prisoner is momentarily lost, uncertain what to do next. Then a familiar vehicle appears – his Lotus 7, as seen in all the opening sequences. It is driven by a striking, angular woman, Mrs. Butterworth (Georgina Cookson – an actor who played a small role at Mme. Engadine's party in *A. B. and C.* What is this woman from The Prisoner's dream doing driving his car? I can only suggest two answers: 1. that it was a prophetic dream, implanted by Village sleep scientists so as to predispose Number 6 towards Mrs. Butterworth; or 2. that casting director Tobias-Shaw just liked the actor and persuaded McGoohan they should use her twice, in different roles, as in a stage play. The same issue will occur again, shortly).

The Prisoner tells Mrs. Butterworth the licence and vehicle identification number of his car, adding 'I know every nut and bolt and cog. I built it with my own hands.' Fascinated by her unshaven visitor, she invites him in. (All this is very different from the script, in which 1 Buckingham Place is divided into apartments, and The Prisoner breaks into his former flat. In the script Mrs. Butterworth is much less of a character, there is no fearsome maid, and the Lotus has simply been sitting in the garage. Presumably, the dialogue between McGoohan and Cookson was improvised. It is more lively and original than what was on the page.)

The Prisoner tells Mrs Butterworth his name is 'Smith. Peter... Smith'. He devours a plate of sandwiches and an entire fruitcake and borrows back his Lotus, promising to return it the next day – his birthday. He retraces the title sequence to the parking garage, walks down the corridor, and confronts the hapless bureaucrat (George Markstein) in his map-filled office. In the next scene he is talking to an old colleague, Colonel James (Donald Sinden), and the Colonel's suspicious assistant, Thorpe.

(Here the casting train-wreck occurs: the actor playing Thorpe is none other than Patrick Cargill, the vicious Number 2 from *Hammer into Anvil.* Now, there is nothing wrong with casting the same actor in a series of roles within one show or series. Lindsay Anderson, who professed to dislike *The Prisoner*, would do exactly the same in *O Lucky Man!* But if one is going to do this, one should do it from the beginning, and make a point of it. Unexpectedly recycling one marginal actor – Cookson – may work well; but to do it twice – especially with Cargill – smacks of carelessness, or of desperate, eleventh-hour decision-making. Not that Cargill is a bad actor. He is excellent. But the very fact that he was so good as the depraved and paranoiac Number 2 in *Hammer into Anvil* means – to this director, at least – that someone else should have been cast in the relatively minor role of Thorpe, the suspicious bureaucrat. If you are going to recycle actors, you should do it frequently and consistently, as in *O Lucky Man!*)

Over drinks in Whitehall, Colonel James and Thorpe study Number 6's photographs, his log, and a copy of the *Tally Ho!* James acknowledges they have 'a mutual problem'. Thorpe distrusts The Prisoner and thinks he has been turned by the Russians. The Prisoner, given his experiences, has every reason to distrust Thorpe and indeed the entire British Establishment. But he apparently convinces James, who assigns Number 6 a military team to pinpoint the location of The Village. Based on his log, they decide it must be on the coast of Morocco, or South-West Portugal, or Southern Spain. Now The Prisoner seems to be receiving every assistance. Dressed in a flight suit, he prepares to board a military jet, whose pilot tells him they will sweep the coasts and refuel at Gibraltar. Number 6 heads for the aircraft as a Milkman enters the crew quarters, delivering pintas from his van. Thorpe and James watch as the plane taxis away.

THORPE: 'Interesting fellow.'

COL. JAMES: 'He's an old, old friend, who never gives up.'

The jet sweeps the coasts, and in due course Number 6 spots The Village. He orders the pilot to close in for a closer look. But his assigned, moustachioed pilot is not at the controls: too late he realises that the plane is flown by *the Milkman*, who calls out 'Be seeing you!' and ejects him. Number 6 is parachuted back down to the beach beside The Village, where the black cat awaits his return.

Number 6 walks through The Village in his flight suit. All is still and quiet, as before. But when he enters his cottage, the water starts to flow, the kettle boils, and Mrs Butterworth – the New Number 2 – enters with his birthday cake, wishing him 'Many Happy Returns'. Outside, the Villagers are marching around the main square, the sun is shining, and the band is playing, as in days of yore.

WHAT HAVE WE LEARNED?

A lot. Let's start with the smaller stuff. Once again, The Prisoner demonstrates himself to be a master at fabricating things. He handcrafts another sailing vessel, scratchbuilds a compass, and tells Mrs. Butterworth that he built his Lotus 7 from the ground up. These are not secret agent skills. In 1967, James Bond was associated with the Aston Martin DB5, a much larger and more heavily-engineered British sports car. It was delivered to him by M's technology department in the movie *Goldfinger*, complete with revolving number plates, an ejector seat, and a pop-up bulletproof shield. As a kid I had the Corgi model – it was a fun little toy, good for ramming other toy cars and ejecting plastic cowboys. But there was never any suggestion that Bond, the top British secret agent, had built the thing himself. Who ever saw Bond with dirty hands, changing his own oil? What I'm getting at, as I'm sure the reader is aware, is that Bond was a spy, and Number 6 was, before he resigned, a *mechanical engineer*.

What kind of engineering he did we shall learn in our study of the final episode, *Fall Out*.

Now, on to who runs The Village. *Many Happy Returns* suggests that the place is owned and operated by the British, just like the Scottish colony for burned-out spies which Markstein heard about. In *The Chimes of Big Ben*, The Prisoner's interrogators faked two rooms in an attempt to trick him. But there is no question of faking the city of London, and no way the Russians or the Chinese – or even the Americans – could pull off an operation of this size and scale without the knowledge of the 'home team'. The events of this episode are clearly orchestrated by Number 6's former colleagues in the British government/secret state, as is his enforced return to The Village in time for his birthday. Colonel James is in on the whole show; he debriefs The Prisoner, assigns him a Royal Navy Commander and an RAF Group Captain to assist, and provides a military jet to conduct his search. The substitution of the Milkman for the RAF pilot is presumably to keep said pilot from learning classified information: the location of The Village.

(To play devil's advocate, one could argue that the Milkman business is meant to depict The Village acting independently of Her Majesty's Government, and to suggest that only the Milkman and Mrs. Butterworth are in on the plot. But that begs too many questions. If Thorpe and Colonel James are on the level, they will know the jig is up as soon as the assigned pilot recovers from the sleeping gas, or, at the latest, when The Prisoner fails to return. Since they have photographs of The Village and claim to know roughly where it is, they can find it for themselves and rescue Number 6 with relative ease.)

Is The Village really in Northern Morocco or Southern Spain or Portugal? Not necessarily. I assume that The Prisoner has been under the influence of yet more sinister drugs – so ubiquitous that their involvement in the narrative and his fractured interpretation of reality can be taken as givens – which have distorted his sense of time and space. Adrift at sea, or in the back of the jet fighter, The Prisoner relies on what his former colleague has told him: that he has sailed in a straight line for 25 days, that they will surveil the Spanish coast and refuel in Gibraltar. The reality is quite different, as we shall see.

14

Episode Fourteen

DO NOT FORSAKE ME OH MY DARLING

With the completion of *Many Happy Returns*, the first season of *The Prisoner* was done. McGoohan departed immediately for the States, to act in *Ice Station Zebra*. And Lew Grade gave word that, after four more episodes, the series would be shut down. But the show faced an even more immediate and serious problem than its impending closure. How to shoot an episode without McGoohan?

Vincent Tilsley, who had written *The Chimes of Big Ben*, was given the difficult assignment, and he didn't like being told that the lead actor would be absent, and that there should be no scenes set in Portmeirion. Nevertheless, he came up with an idea which fitted very well: another misuse-of-science/science-fiction episode, in which The Prisoner's mind would be transferred into someone else's body. *Face Unknown* would be the last episode directed by Pat Jackson. While heavily reliant on recycled footage from the first season, and on stock shots of European travel, it's a fine episode. Tilsley was a decent writer and he did his best, still relying on the brief Markstein had given him. Markstein had now departed the series, due to unresolvable creative differences with McGoohan. But for all Tilsley knew, Number 6 was a spy in the *Danger Man* mould. He wrote accordingly. He had not read the scripts of the previous episodes, and so his screenplay contradicts them in numerous ways. It could all have been a disaster – but it is not. That this wild-card, improbable episode works so well is thanks to the presence of an underrated actor, Nigel Stock, in the McGoohan role.

Face Unknown was shot during McGoohan's absence late in 1967, and renamed *Do Not Forsake Me Oh My Darling* by producer Tomblin, who poached the title from another *Prisoner* script, shortly to be filmed. It begins in an unusual way, with a prologue in which various British Civil Service mandarins – presumably high-ranking spies – puzzle over a series of slides projected on a screen: the Eiffel Tower, Loch Ness, Beachy Head. One of them, Sir Charles Portland (John Wentworth), remarks, 'Not an inspired photographer... but a brilliant scientist.' The mandarins study slide Number 6, a portrait of an elderly, white-haired man. Sir Charles suspects a coded message is hidden within the slides – a message which will lead them to the individual they seek: 'Seltzman'.

This is followed by the standard opening credits sequence – curtailed early for some aerial footage of The Village as a helicopter comes in to land. Number 2 (Clifford Evans) watches Number 6 on his surveillance screen, and welcomes an erect, besuited Englishman without a Village number badge: the

Colonel (Nigel Stock). The Butler has prepared the usual ritual of breakfast, which the Colonel declines. He wants to know what his duties are, immediately, having been sent here 'by the highest authority'. (In his script, Tilsley describes the Colonel specifically as a stupid character, but Stock doesn't play it that way. His Colonel is straight to the point, no-nonsense, and nobody's fool.) Number 2 asks if he is familiar with Professor Jacob Seltzman.

NUMBER 2: 'Dr. Seltzman is a great neurologist who became fascinated with the study of thought transference.'

COLONEL: 'I've actually seen it done. In India.'

NUMBER 2: '... where Seltzman studied for many years.'

Number 2 reveals that Seltzman has discovered how to transmit the mind of one man into the body of another, using a mixture of yogic and scientific techniques. The Colonel refuses to believe it, and asks where Seltzman is. Therein lies the problem, and the episode's plot. No one knows where he is. 'The only man who may, because he had the last contact with him... is our friend.' They both watch Number 6, pacing back and forth in his cottage. The Colonel still remains dubious.

NUMBER 2: 'Colonel, if I had told you ten years ago that we could fly a rocket around the Moon, would you have believed that?

COLONEL: 'No, I suppose not.'

NUMBER 2: '... you must be aware that all major powers have in their prisons one or two of each other's spies.'

COLONEL: 'Yes.'

NUMBER 2: 'From time to time, diplomatic swaps take place. Imagine the power we would have if the spy we returned had the mind of our choosing. *We could break the security of any nation.*'

Yes indeed! Seltzman's invention is the NSA's wet dream! Number 2 shows the Colonel The Village's 'Amnesia Room' – in which unwanted recollections are technologically erased from the subject's mind. Here it is possible to wipe out memories of The Village and return former prisoners to circulation. Number 2 proudly gives the Colonel a demonstration of 'the Seltzman Machine', while (in a scene requiring a second-unit shoot in Portmeirion, involving McGoohan's double), Number 6 is dragged from his cottage by 'White Helmets' and driven to The Hospital.

Next morning, Number 6 wakes up in his old house, in London. He has forgotten The Village and what took place there. He studies his agenda and the portrait of Janet, his fiancée. Then he looks in the mirror. He sees the face of Nigel Stock. Flashbacks follow, recalling fragments of what has occurred: clips from *Arrival* and *Free for All*. Then the doorbell rings, and Janet (Zena Walker) is at the door. Naturally, she doesn't recognise him. He pretends to be a friend of The Prisoner, who he learns vanished a year ago, on the eve of Janet's birthday. Uncertain that he can convince her, he says The Prisoner is on a mission, and promises to bring a message from him to her birthday party. When she is gone, he smashes the mirror with his fist.

Janet goes to see her father, Sir Charles, in his grand office. He denies sending The Prisoner on any mission, and asks who this friend is. Janet says the man is 'perfectly ordinary'. Meanwhile The Prisoner drives to his old employer's office – now occupied by a new bureaucrat, John Peregrine Danvers (Patrick Jordan) and demands to see Sir Charles. He reels off Danvers' CV – including the embarrassing fact that this mandarin-in-training is from Bootle, Merseyside. Another bureaucrat, Villiers (James Bree), appears and asks his name.

NUMBER 6: 'Code, or real?'

VILLIERS: 'Code.'

NUMBER 6: 'In France, Duval. In Germany, Schmidt. You would know me best as ZM73. And your code number is PR12.'

When Number 6 mentions the Seltzman process, and shows Villiers his actual photograph, he is taken to see Sir Charles. He recalls personal family details and the occasion when he asked for permission to marry Janet. Sir Charles remarks that all this information could have been extracted under sedation or hypnosis (two of the techniques which we have frequently seen The Village use), and that he cannot possibly trust Number 6. Instead, he will have him watched and followed.

NUMBER 6: 'That's a waste of somebody's time.'

SIR CHARLES: 'He'll be paid for it.'

What bitter irony! Back in London, in the wrong body, The Prisoner continues to receive The Village treatment: identified by a code number, to be surveilled wherever he goes. And how frank of Sir Charles to remark that this is all a business which people get paid to do, just as Number 6 once received a salary in London and accumulated Work Units in The Village. The Village may not be Sir Charles' operation but he certainly understands its methods, and practises them himself. A homing device is attached to the Lotus, which is followed by a plain-clothes man, Potter (Frederick Abbott).

In a voiceover, The Prisoner asks himself where Seltzman is. 'Did he perfect the reversion process? If he didn't … it's a pity.' He wants to return to his own body. What he doesn't know is that, in trying to find Seltzman, he will be following the mission Number 2 has assigned to him. Shadowed by Potter and a Village undertaker, he goes home, studies his handwriting, and discovers it is still the same. Encouraged, he opens the safe behind his television, where, like a good Englishman, he has stashed several stacks of US greenbacks for an emergency. He attends Janet's party, and asks her for a slip of paper The Prisoner left with her for safekeeping. He waits for her in the arbour (formerly the Professor's garden, and Mme. Engadine's). Janet brings him the paper, a receipt. They kiss for a long time. Now she knows who he is.

(At this point, if I was The Prisoner, I would stay put in London in the body of Nigel Stock, and move in with Janet. It's a decent body, with excellent posture and a nice, ordinary face. I could prove to her father who I was via handwriting analysis, and get my old job back. But as The Prisoner has been programmed to seek out Seltzman, and is not in control of his actions, I digress.)

Pursued by Potter, The Prisoner visits a camera shop on Victoria Colonnade. He hands in the receipt and receives a box of slides. He learns that, due to a 'clerical error', someone has already collected and returned the slides. He requests a passport photograph. Back home, he superimposes four transparencies selected via a code involving Seltzman's name, and using special lenses learns that Seltzman is in Kandersfeld, Austria. Dogged by Potter, The Prisoner heads for Dover and boards the car ferry. There follows a sequence of stock European travel shots and rear-screen projection driving. Accordion music plays (this must be France, right?). A polka plays as we near Kandersfeld.

Number 6 shows Seltzman's picture to a waiter, who recognises him as 'Herr Hallen', the local barber. He meets Seltzman (Hugo Schuster) in the barbershop, and tries to convince him that he is a victim of the Seltzman process. He runs into the same problem he encountered with Sir Charles: 'But everything I tell you can be countered by you, by saying I've extracted the information by fair means or foul.' Fortunately, the handwriting test convinces the scientist.

Seltzman confirms that the reversal process exists – and could be dangerous.

Potter arrives and pulls a gun. He and Number 6 fight, only to be gassed unconscious by a green-clad Village operative. The Professor and The Prisoner are returned to The Village – which adds yet another big name to its roster of scientist-prisoners. But Seltzman will not be recruited, and an unscripted debate occurs:

SELTZMAN: 'Surely neither of us wants to prolong this interview.'

NUMBER 2: 'Life has not taught you sweet resignation.'

SELTZMAN: 'Nor has it for many other scientists. Rutherford, for example. How he must regret having split the atom.'

But this Number 2 is one of the smartest ones. He points out that, as the inventor of the process, the Professor has a 'slight responsibility' to Number 6, his brain stuck in the Colonel's head while his body twitches on a laboratory gurney. Seltzman relents, and agrees to reverse the process. But when it takes place, he plugs himself into the apparatus and is apparently killed. The Colonel departs aboard the helicopter as Seltzman breathes his last words to Number 2.

SELTZMAN: 'You assured me that he was in good health. You must contact Number 1 and tell him... I did my duty.'

Too late, Number 2 realises what has happened. Rising from his gurney, Number 6 confirms that Seltzman has switched bodies with the Colonel, and escaped.

WHAT HAVE WE LEARNED?

Do Not Forsake Me is a tremendous critique of so-called 'intelligence' methods of extracting information. Drugs, hypnosis and psychological pressure can induce people to say anything: so nothing anyone says can be relied upon. In the Colonel's body, Number 6 is like a torture victim in Abu Ghraib prison: the forces of freedom may extract information from him, but they cannot rely on it, because people who are being tortured will tell their torturer whatever he or she appears to want to hear. This is old news, of course. But it's a pity more American politicians and spooks didn't watch *The Prisoner*. They might have learned something: that coerced 'intelligence' is worthless.

In the context of the series, *Do Not Forsake Me* provides indisputable evidence that Number 6 is a British spy. Tilsley had been briefed by Markstein to this effect, and both his scripts reflect his briefing. This, of course, confounds my thesis that Number 6 is an engineer. More seriously, it contradicts much that has occurred in previous episodes.

Its principal departure is the introduction of two new characters: Janet and Sir Charles. Both pose major problems of consistency, in a series which is otherwise very consistent. *The Prisoner* developed from episode to episode. As each new show was complete, more was known about Number 6 and about The Village. But *Do Not Forsake Me*, in which The Prisoner again returns to London, entirely contradicts *Many Happy Returns*. If The Prisoner had a loving fiancée called

Janet, why didn't he look for her in that previous episode? Janet lives in London. He could have gone to her house, rather than bother Mrs. Butterworth, a person he had no reason to trust. When Thorpe doubted his story, why didn't they contact Janet's father, the secret service mandarin? For that matter, when Colonel J in *The Chimes of Big Ben* questioned his veracity, why didn't The Prisoner suggest they call Sir Charles?

Even if the order of episodes is reversed, the same problems remain. Either Janet and Sir Charles are part of the entire *Prisoner* story – like Rover and the Supervisor and the Butler – or they are not. Vincent Tilsley wrote well, but his failure to read the other scripts crippled his episode's ability to fit into a coherent narrative. The previous thirteen shows developed the character of Number 6 as a lone wolf without romantic ties, with extraordinary engineering and fabricating skills. Suddenly, in the fourteenth episode, he is a tuxedoed spy with a beautiful fiancée.

This will not fly. And the episode's conclusion – in which Seltzman's mind escapes in the Colonel's body, aboard The Village helicopter – is ridiculous. As we well know, all Village vehicles are drones which can be operated from the Control Room. There is no way a prisoner can escape aboard that chopper. Number 6 tried to do so in *Arrival*, and completely failed.

That *Do Not Forsake Me* works so well is due, I believe, to the presence of the 'perfectly ordinary' Nigel Stock. Stock was one of those familiar British actors who seemed to be in everything. Among his many roles, he portrayed Winston Churchill, Mr. Pickwick, and Vyacheslav Molotov. He was best known on British TV as Doctor Watson to Peter Cushing's Sherlock Holmes. Cushing was one of the best actors ever to play Holmes, and needless to say he overshadowed Stock in the series. That is as it should be, for Watson is Holmes' foil. There is no way Watson can overshadow Holmes. Stock's genius was to imbue a relatively thankless role – Sherlock Holmes' slower-witted stooge, in this case – with character and integrity. For an actor, this was harder than playing Holmes, and, perhaps, more rewarding. Now, in *The Prisoner*, we see him playing Patrick McGoohan's character. It's interesting to contrast their acting styles.

As an actor, McGoohan seems to have two speeds, like my old Chevy Impala: *low*, in which he is entirely credible, low-key, and frequently charming; and *high*, in which his voice suddenly leaps in pitch, he often shouts, and he tends to smash things. In 1968, he told *TV Guide*, 'I like working under pressure. I, unluckily, only have two gears. Very low and very high. I wish I could cultivate the middle gear, but I can't.' McGoohan was talking about himself, I think, but he describes his performing style as well. And he does show less nuance than the non-star actor, seven-speed Stock. The scene where The Prisoner, in Stock's body, smashes the mirror is classic McGoohan. The scene in which he kisses his beloved, and thus convinces her who he is, is pure Stock. Stock remarked that he and Zena Walker had kissed in several previous shows. McGoohan, famously, didn't kiss on screen at all. Stock and Walker liked each other and were at ease. Actors generally admired Stock, and enjoyed working with him. Some actors loved to work with McGoohan, others didn't. Some said his presence filled a room, others just found it grandstand-y and intimidating. Several thought his refusal to play romantic scenes plain silly. A couple complained that McGoohan 'lost it' in fight sequences, and started fighting for real, an unpardonable actor's crime.

As a writer and director, McGoohan did the best work of the series – indeed, some of the finest writing and directing episodic television has ever seen. It would be miraculous if he was also the best actor in the series. He was the most popular, of course, and the highest-paid. He was the star. But stars and actors are different things.

Stock said, regarding the episode, 'I had to think of myself as Pat (McGoohan) all the time, behaving in the way he would be doing. Fortunately I've worked with him several times, so I've been able to imitate several of his characteristics like the way he flicks his fingers and touches his face.' None of this face-touching or finger-flicking made it into the episode. McGoohan was unhappy with the first cut of *Do Not Forsake Me*, and re-edited it extensively – perhaps removing shots in which Stock mimicked his acting. Yet Stock still got to 'play' McGoohan: as the Colonel, Stock stands bolt-upright; when he breaks the mirror he slumps, as McGoohan often does.

Despite the unreliability of this episode, I enjoy it a lot and find it fascinating that Number 6's British bosses only begin to believe him when he uses their alphanumeric code names: ZM73 and PR12. Despite his insistence at the start of every show that he is *not* a number, The Prisoner has once again opted to identify himself by numbers, rather than his real name. For the mandarins, these numbers are 'secrets' and hence more trustworthy than names. The Prisoner was a number long before they rendered him.

Lastly, I would discount as irrelevant the dying Colonel's characterisation of Number 1 as 'him'. This is the only such reference in the series thus far. It was not scripted. In the shooting script, Number 2 addresses his telephonic master as 'Number 1' – dialogue not in the finished show. Probably Tilsley, briefed by Markstein, believed Number 1 to be a Dr No-type master villain. But there's no evidence elsewhere that Number 1 is a he, or human at all.

15

Episode Fifteen

LIVING IN HARMONY

Though he hadn't written a screenplay before, Ian Rakoff proposed a script idea to Patrick McGoohan in the MGM canteen: a Western episode, in which Number 6 would be a sheriff who quit his job in a corrupt and lawless town. McGoohan liked the idea, and encouraged him to develop it. Rakoff titled his script *Do Not Forsake Me Oh My Darling*, after the theme song of the American Western *High Noon*. In his book, he recounts the grisly day when he was scheduled to attend a script meeting with his star. McGoohan arrived more than two hours late, straight from a meeting with Lew Grade. He paced his office furiously, complaining incoherently about Grade.

> 'The problem was that Grade was letting him down, and not behaving as he should, McGoohan said. Lew Grade didn't understand. Of everyone, he felt that Lew should be the understanding one. He was no different from all the others. George Markstein was briefly referred to. The context eluded me...
>
> '... that's the sort of thing you should be writing about [McGoohan told him]. The power, the politics, the money behind it. He's the one that's in control. He's the one that says stop and go. We've thirteen episodes near completion, and four more to go. After that, who knows? It could all end with the 26-episode run. It could all end tomorrow, even today.'

Was Grade's decision to end the series – or his disinclination to extend it – reversible? McGoohan apparently thought he might still change the financier's mind. Maybe there would be two complete seasons of *The Prisoner* after all. Rakoff asked McGoohan what he thought of his Western script. McGoohan looked at him blankly. He shook his head, and began to rage again, accusing Rakoff of surrendering to despair. For two hours, McGoohan ranted, not discussing the script at all. Then, as Rakoff was getting up to leave, McGoohan told him they would be using his screenplay. 'You've already got most of it down there. It's a proper Western. It's different, but it fits into The Village effectively.'

Further script meetings were scheduled, but little discussion took place. Rakoff regretted Markstein's departure, and disliked David Tomblin, the producer, who was increasingly present. Tomblin decided that Rakoff's title would be needed for the Nigel Stock episode. Rakoff said fine, and came up with *Living in Harmony* as an alternative. Then McGoohan told him he was leaving for Hollywood, intimating that this was to secure money to fund the last four episodes. Tomblin told Rakoff the same thing, but, as already observed, this cannot have been so: Grade's company, ITC, was paying for the series. Leo McKern remarked that McGoohan was obsessed with money, so it's unlikely that he was earning his three-quarters-of-a-million-dollar movie salary simply to give it to Lew Grade. Rakoff had assumed that McGoohan would direct the Western episode, but once he was gone, Tomblin announced that he, Tomblin, would be directing it. As it turned out, he also gave himself the writing credit, plus one additional title card, 'From a Story by David Tomblin and Ian L. Rakoff'. McGoohan returned just in time to act in the episode, which was directed, produced, and 'written' by Tomblin.

This was Rakoff's first crack at being a professional screenwriter. He was demoralised and felt screwed over by the experience. Yet the resulting episode is strikingly good. For all his preproduction manoeuvring, Tomblin did an excellent job directing, and for the first time Brendan Stafford's lighting involved deep shadows, and his shooting was liberated by taking the camera off the tripod. Their model was clearly the Italian Western, with its dynamic camera, big closeups, minimal dialogue, sadistic violence, and archetypal characters, many of whom lack names. Indeed, they were so successful at emulating a good, nihilistic Italian Western that neither the American nor the French networks would screen it.

There is no pre-credits sequence. There is no *Prisoner* title.

Instead we see a lone figure, riding across a huge plain. Next we are in a marshal's office, where a lawman (McGoohan) turns in his sheriff's badge and his gun. (This is Italian Western territory. Western sheriffs were not assistant marshals – they were county peace officers; marshals were either federal officers or city policemen. But the Italians cared nothing for these distinctions, and obviously Tomblin felt the same way.)

When next we encounter him, the lawman is on foot, carrying his saddle, like Django in Sergio Corbucci's film. He is accosted by six toughs in cowboy outfits who beat him up and dump him in a Western settlement called Harmony (the viewer will not be astonished to learn that Harmony is the backlot at MGM, where another French village set had been created for the film *Eye of the Devil*. Jack Shampan and crew provided it with Western signage and facades).

As the lawman dusts himself off, an impressively toothsome Mexican (Larry Taylor) directs him to the saloon. When the lawman enters, the pianist stops playing. This was an old Western cliché long abandoned by the Americans, recently resurrected by Sergio Leone in *For a Few Dollars More*. When saloon girl Cathy (Valerie French) offers the lawman a drink, a top-hatted, mute young gunfighter known as the Kid (Alexis Kanner) shoots the glass off the bar. The lawman takes a second whiskey, turns, and punches the Kid to the barroom floor.

Playing solitaire at a back table is a well-dressed, older man, the Judge (David Bauer). The Judge knows who the lawman is and invites him to join him. He offers him a job.

LAWMAN: 'I'm not for hire.'

JUDGE: 'You turned in your badge.'

LAWMAN: 'And my gun.'

JUDGE: 'What were your reasons?'

LAWMAN: 'My reasons.'

So, like The Prisoner, the lawman will neither reveal his motivation for resigning nor sign on as a full-time employee. And, like The Prisoner, he finds that leaving this new home is difficult, if not impossible. At the livery stable, he's told a horse will cost him $5,000. He is pursued by a group of townspeople, who exhort him to live in Harmony. When he declines, the Mexican insists that the town has been insulted and incites the mob to beat him up. The lawman is rescued by the Judge's armed coterie, who escort him to the jail. The Judge is already there, making coffee. He puts the lawman in 'protective custody'. To appease the mob, he gives them another prisoner, Johnson, who is promptly lynched.

The lynching of Johnson is classic Italian Western stuff – hand-held camera, point-of-view shots, grotesque faces featured in extreme closeups. Cathy turns out to be Johnson's sister: she is the only principal character in the episode who has a name. The rest are known by monikers – the Kid, the Judge – or, like McGoohan's character, they have no name at all. This, at the time, was perceived as an Italian Western trait. In fact, in the *Dollars* films, Clint Eastwood's character always had a name – Joe, Manco, Blondie – but no matter: for their theatrical release, United Artists was promoting Eastwood's bounty killer as 'The Man With No Name'.

In jail, the Kid eyes the lawman and gets drunk. Cathy brings him another bottle of whiskey, resists his advances, and palms the jailhouse keys. These she slips to the lawman, who breaks out and steals a horse. He does not get far. Lassoed by the Judge's men, he is dragged back to Harmony. In the saloon, the Judge stages an impromptu trial – not of the lawman, but of Cathy, for helping him to escape. A jury of his saloon patrons finds her guilty, and she is jailed. The Judge tells the lawman, 'When you work for me, I'll let her go.'

A familiar *Prisoner* scenario is developing: the protagonist, unwilling to play by Village/Harmony rules, is co-opted when a woman's life is threatened. The Kid attempts to provoke him, and fails. When the Kid turns his attentions to Cathy, the lawman relents and agrees to wear the sheriff's badge – but not his gun. Accosted by thugs, the lawman bests them in a fist fight. Oddly, he fails to arrest them, and repairs to the jail alone.

That night, in the saloon, the Kid stalks Cathy and kills a drunken cowboy for flirting with her. Since the hapless cowpoke drew his pistol first, the lawman cannot arrest the Kid. A concerned citizen appears and begs him to clean up the town. In the next scene the citizen lies dead in the sheriff's chair. The lawman tells Cathy to meet him on the edge of town at nightfall. He overcomes the Judge's guards, but Cathy does not appear. She has been accosted by the Kid, who – when his advances are once again rebuffed – strangles her. The lawman returns to town and finds her body. Framed in a classic Western silhouette, he buries her at dawn. In the jail, he washes his hands, puts on the gunbelt, and takes off the badge. Outside, the Kid waits for a showdown. The Kid draws first – and the lawman shoots him dead.

In the saloon, the Judge panics, insisting that the lawman must continue to work for him. 'Nobody walks out on me!' When the lawman tries to do exactly that, a gunfight erupts. He kills three of the Judge's henchmen – only to be shot twice by the Judge. He collapses, dying, on the wooden floor…

… and wakes, clad in his Number 6 blazer, wearing a pair of headphones and a portable microphone. He thinks he sees the Judge, aiming his Derringer – but the Judge is a cardboard cutout, not a man. Outside, a cutout of the Kid lies in the street. A cardboard horse is tethered to a hitching rail. The lawman hears the music of The Village band. Harmony turns out to be a movie set, built on a hillside overlooking The Village. Number 6/the lawman marches back to confront his persecutors in the Dome.

There, the Judge, the Kid and Cathy await him, dressed in casual Village attire. They too wear microphones and headsets:

they are Number 2, Number 8, and Number 22 respectively. All this The Prisoner understands. He leaves without addressing them. Number 22/Cathy is genuinely remorseful and bursts into tears. Number 2/The Judge and Number 8/The Kid discuss the failure of their virtual reality mindgame.

NUMBER 8: 'Interesting, that he can separate fact from fantasy so quickly.'

NUMBER 2: 'I told you he was different. I knew it wouldn't work. Fill him with hallucinatory drugs. Put him in a dangerous environment. Talk to him through microphones.'

NUMBER 8: 'It's always worked. And it would have worked this time, if you – '

NUMBER 2: 'But it didn't, did it? Give him love – take it away – Isolate him. Make him kill. Then face him with death. He'll crack. Break him, even in his mind, and the rest will be easy. I should never have listened to you.'

NUMBER 8: 'It would have worked. If you had kept your head and not created the crisis too soon.'

NUMBER 2: 'How could I control it? You said yourself we would get involved.'

And indeed they have. While Number 2 and Number 8 argue – clearly Number 8 is a scientist/psychologist in his own right – Number 22 bursts into tears. As a result of the experiment, she has fallen in love with Number 6.

That night Number 22 returns to the Western set saloon. Number 8 follows her. Both of them have been more influenced by the drugs and the intense experience than they anticipated. Channelling the Kid, Number 8 stalks Number 22 and, reliving the experiment, strangles her. The Prisoner, too, returns to the Western set. He hears Number 8's insane screams and races to the saloon. But he is too late to save Number 22, who dies in his arms. Number 2 arrives aboard a Moke. Number 8, thinking 'The Judge' has come to punish him, commits suicide by jumping from the balcony.

In classic Western style, Number 6 leaves Number 2 to deal with the corpses, and pushes his way out through the batwing doors.

WHAT HAVE WE LEARNED?

Nothing new that I can discern. The Prisoner has used neither spy tradecraft nor engineering expertise. We already know that The Village uses psychoactive drugs to control and manipulate its residents. And we can be fairly sure that David Tomblin took the principal crew of *Living in Harmony* to see *For a Few Dollars More*, which opened in England early in 1967. Sergio Leone's visual and moral aesthetics permeate *Living in Harmony*.

Perhaps the most interesting aspect of this episode is the American (and French) reaction to it. In both countries, when *The Prisoner* was first screened, *Living in Harmony* wasn't shown. Why? There's been speculation that it was overly violent – or that it was a commentary on the Vietnam War. The latter response I find hard to treat seriously. The work of Peter Watkins in *Culloden* and *The War Game* might reasonably be viewed as a commentary on American foreign policy, on Vietnam, and on the coming nuclear war. *Living in Harmony*, for all its virtues, is a cowboy film. It's also been suggested that the reference to hallucinogenic drugs caused the episode to be banned – but several earlier episodes of *The Prisoner* involved drugs, and all were screened without cuts. My suspicion is that *Living in Harmony* was simply too genre-breaking for the American and French TV gatekeepers. As a whole, the *Prisoner* series was already 'out there'. *Living in Harmony* went even further into the misty beyond, and, as it was also so visually different from the other episodes, it became something the gatekeepers' unfathomably shallow minds could focus on.

In 1967, Italian Westerns had already proved hugely popular with audiences worldwide – but not with mainstream film critics, who clung to the racist notion that only Americans could, or should, make cowboy films. TV gatekeepers were even more conservative than mainstream film reviewers (if such a thing is possible) and an Italian Western *Prisoner* was simply beyond their intellectual and emotional capacities. In that way, *Living in Harmony* is the most transgressive *Prisoner* story, though far from its most original episode.

16

Episode Sixteen

THE GIRL WHO WAS DEATH

The Girl Who Was Death was shot in late October and early November 1967 (though parts were completed during the *Fall Out* shoot). It was written by Terence Feely, 'from an idea by David Tomblin'. Tomblin also directed. Feely had written the excellent *Schizoid Man*, but his tone here is entirely different. This is the first, and only, comic *Prisoner* episode. Justine Lord, who played the eponymous *Girl*, observed that 'David Tomblin seemed to decide things on the day… Patrick didn't join us for a couple of weeks.' Indeed, the episode seems to have been constructed so that most of the exteriors could be played by McGoohan's double, Maher, or his stand-in, Geoff Morrow. McGoohan is present for some street scenes and shots on the MGM backlot, but most of his 'exteriors' are rear projections.

Perhaps *Ice Station Zebra* had summoned him back to Los Angeles. All this infelicity – the assumed and discarded disguises, the unconvincing intercutting of rear-projection McGoohan with on-location Lord – works to assist this bizarre episode, adding to its artificiality and theatrical charm.

The story is bookended (and commercial-break-ended) with pages from a children's picture book. It begins in an English village, where a cricket match is in progress. The moustachioed Colonel Hawke-English is batting. Sonia (Justine Lord), a glamorous woman in white, substitutes the cricket ball for a bomb, and Hawke-English is killed.

On a London street, Mr X (Patrick McGoohan) reads a newspaper report of the murder. He looks somewhat like the working-class cartoon character Andy Capp, with his flat cap and raincoat. But in fact he is a secret agent. Another agent by the name of Potter (Christopher Benjamin), who was keeping score at the match, is now disguised as a shoe-shine boy. He tells X that Hawke-English was pursuing 'a crazy scientist … building a super-rocket to destroy London.' Now X is to take over the mission, where Hawke-English left off. Sonia, disguised as a mannequin, listens from the window of a fashion shop.

Back at the cricket match, X takes the wicket in place of the Colonel. He wears false whiskers. Sonia tries to kill him with another exploding cricket ball, but he tosses the bomb into the bushes. Finding a note inviting him to his local pub, X goes there, orders a pint, and discovers – via a message etched on the bottom of his glass – that his beer is poisoned. Quickly he downs a succession of brandies and sweet liqueurs. He vomits up the poison in the gents' and finds another note, on the towel rack, inviting him to Benny's Turkish Baths. There, Sonia traps him in a steam machine. Escaping with ease – and clad in a full Sherlock Holmes outfit with deerstalker – X pursues Sonia to

Barney's Boxing Booth, at the fairground, and is dragged into a boxing match with an Irishman, 'Killer' Kaminski (Michael Brennan), who advises him to meet Sonia in the Tunnel of Love.

In the Tunnel, Sonia tries to kill him with an exploding transistor radio. He pursues her around the rides (Alexis Kanner enjoys an uncredited cameo as her photographer boyfriend). A sports car chase through the countryside follows. Sonia is able to manipulate X's sense of reality so that his car and the road seem to spin around him. But he manages to follow her to the deserted hamlet of Witchwood (which looks nothing like an English Cotswold village and entirely like the French backlot at MGM). Sonia taunts X via the public address system. He pursues her through a butcher's, where an automated machine gun awaits him; a baker's, where he falls into a pit of electrified spikes; and a candlestick maker's, where explosive candles releasing cyanide gas almost snuff out his life.

Sonia attempts to kill X with a Gatling gun, a shower of mortars, and a bazooka, then departs in her helicopter. But X jumps aboard the chopper and follows her to a lighthouse on the English coast – the same lighthouse we saw in *Many Happy Returns*. In a bunker beneath the lighthouse are pictures of Napoleon Bonaparte and his Empress, Josephine. X discovers the mad professor, Schnipps (Kenneth Griffith), and his crew, dressed in Napoleon outfits, and Sonia, his daughter – now clad as Marie Antoinette. He spikes some of the guns and grenades in their armoury, but is captured and tied to a chair in the lighthouse – which, it turns out, is Schnipps' rocket missile. The launch countdown begins.

While Schnipps and Sonia collect his papers, X breaks free and steals their speedboat. They attempt to throw grenades at him, but the doctored grenades explode in their hands, destroying the Lighthouse/Rocket in the nick of time. We cut to the last illustration in the picture book: it looks like a scene from *Moby Dick*, with a lone sailor pursuing a spouting whale.

Then we are back in The Village, in the bedroom of three small children. The Prisoner – no longer costumed as Mr X – closes the book and tells the kids, 'And that is how I saved London from the mad scientist.' In the Dome, Number 2 (Kenneth Griffith) fumes that their gamble that Number 6 'might drop his guard with children' has failed. On the surveillance screen, Number 6 suddenly reappears. He looks at the camera, smiles, and says 'Good night, children, everywhere.'

WHAT HAVE WE LEARNED?

Little. This is a fairy story invented by The Prisoner to entertain The Village children and annoy Number 2. In the first draft script, Schnipps and his crew are all dressed as Adolf Hitler, and greet each other with Nazi salutes. This makes a certain sense, since Hitler did indeed strike London with the V-1 and V-2 missiles, designed for him by his rocket ace, Wernher von Braun. But, despite Mel Brooks and *The Producers*, the idea of multiple comic Hitlers may have seemed impossibly transgressive and outrageous to the gatekeepers at ITC or CBS. Since McGoohan was absent, he was less likely to stick up for Feely's original concept. Hence, perhaps, the tedious, multiple Bonapartes.

Despite its fantasy nature, *The Girl Who Was Death* develops the *Prisoner* narrative in two specific ways: the villain is a rocketeer, and it's the second episode in which Number 6 picks up a gun. As this is a children's story, devised by Number 6, he decides Schnipps' profession – for reasons which will become clearer in the next episode/chapter. And he decides, within the parameters of his fairy tale, to embrace the temptation of firearms – something both he and the series have avoided, until recently.

17

Episode Seventeen
FALL OUT

For Frank Maher, McGoohan's double, the decision to end the series with the seventeenth episode was a complete surprise. 'Pat came to me on Wednesday and said, "We've only got one more show". I said, "What are you talking about?" because we were booked for twenty-six. He said, "That's it!" He went and told the rest of the crew and there had to be a final episode which hadn't been written yet.'

Fall Out is that final episode. It was shot in November 1967. McGoohan wrote and directed it. He had begun writing the script on a flight back from Los Angeles. For him, this final instalment was the continuation of *Once Upon A Time*, which he had also written and directed. It's the third episode in which Leo McKern appears as Number 2. McKern's character had died at the end of *Once Upon A Time*, and in the intervening months, the actor had had a shave and a haircut, and lost some pounds – but, since this was *The Prisoner*, these issues were easily resolved.

Like *Living in Harmony*, *Fall Out* abandons the traditional opening sequence. Instead almost four minutes' worth of flashbacks recall highlights of *Once Upon A Time*. Then we are back in the corridors beneath The Village: the Supervisor is taking Number 6 and the Butler to meet Number 1. Behind a door, they encounter a mannequin with The Prisoner's face and his old suit. 'We thought you'd be happier as yourself,' the Supervisor tells him. Dressed to the nines, Number 6 follows the others down a stone tunnel filled with jukeboxes, all playing The Beatles' *All You Need Is Love*.

(In case this all sounds too lovey-kooly and trippy-dippy, the original script shows this wasn't McGoohan's intention. In the *Fall Out* screenplay, he wrote:

> 'Bring in the strains of *Strawberry Fields*... They proceed along the corridor towards us. It is lined with jukeboxes which blare forth each its own lament: *All You Need Is Love*, *Little Boxes*, *Toot-Toot-Tootsie Goodbye*, *Hello Dolly*, *Yellow Submarine*. Or whatever. There is a moment's predominance for each ditty but eventually they merge into a wailing cacophony.'

McGoohan was unsentimental about the 'ditties' playing on the jukeboxes. Indeed, he was hostile to them. He wanted the sound of mayhem, 'or whatever'. Having experimented with them, he used *All You Need Is Love* on its own. At this stage The Beatles' song doesn't achieve mayhem. Later, it will.)

Number 6, the Butler and the Supervisor enter the largest *Prisoner* set of all: a huge, stalactite-dripping cave, filled with marching armed White Helmets, green-clad surgeons, white-lab-coated scientists at computer stations, a surveillance screen, what appears to be a massive jury box, a podium, and a throne. A man in judge's robes welcomes The Prisoner, while the Supervisor dons a white sheet-like robe and a black-and-white Janus mask, and joins the identically-clad 'Delegates' in the jury box. Identity politics rules them: they are designated as 'Welfare – Pacifists – Activists – Defectors – Reactionists – Nationalists – Youngsters – Identification – Therapy – Education – Entertainment'.

Dominating the room is a huge, silver, smoking tube with a blinking, robotic eye, an intermittent siren, and '1' painted on its fuselage. McGoohan's script describes the massive structure thus: 'Perfectly plain and cylindrical it could be a rocket. Certainly it steams with the vapours of take-off. Also it boasts a modest appellation, being the figure 1 (one) writ large on its side.'

The man in judge's robes – the President – is played by Kenneth Griffith, Number 2 in *The Girl Who Was Death*. So there is character continuity here. Despite his fawning manner, we must conclude that this is another attempt on the part of The Village to subvert or break The Prisoner. The President greets him like a plucky contest winner, declaring that they face a 'democratic crisis', and are 'gathered to resolve the question of revolt'. Again, as in *Free for All*, Number 2 warns of a deficiency in the democratic system, and assumes this is something that The Prisoner would like to fix. The Supervisor advises the President that Number 6 has passed the ultimate test (presumably the Degree Absolute, when McKern's Number 2 successfully pressed him to become a killer).

PRESIDENT: 'Then he must no longer be referred to as Number 6, or a number of any kind. He has gloriously vindicated the right of the individual to be individual. This chamber rises to you, sir.'

From now on, The Prisoner will be known as 'sir'. The President apologises that there is some procedural work to be done before 'the ceremony of transfer of ultimate power' and invites him to take a throne. Uncharacteristically, The Prisoner does so. The Butler joins him on his dais. The barred cage is lowered onto the back of a low loader (unseen for the moment) and the body of an old Number 2 (Leo McKern) is removed and placed on a gurney.

The President declares he will address three specific instances of revolt. The first is the revolt of youth, exemplified by Number 48 (Alexis Kanner), presumably a resuscitated or clone-constructed version of Number 8 in *Living in Harmony*. Like the Kid, Number 48 sports sharp sideburns and a top hat. Emerging from a smoky prison beneath the cave, Number 48 engages in ferocious lingo-banter with the President, then bursts into a rendition of *Dem Dry Bones*, causing panic followed by dancing and clapping among the white-robed Delegates. Thus begins *The Prisoner*'s first, and only, musical number. (I find Kanner somewhat annoying as this embodiment of youth, doing both the Black thing – with the Spiritual song – and the Jesus thing – where an actor throws out his arms, as if crucified, and gazes soulfully at the sky. But actors only do this if directors let them, and presumably Kanner was acting as the director wanted.)

After Number 48 is returned to his smoking prison, McKern's Number 2 is resuscitated by The Village's surgeon/scientists. The revived Number 2 is in a better mood, willingly surrendering his Butler to The Prisoner. Once more, he insists he was a prisoner of The Village, and now regrets his lack of resistance. He watches the playback of himself drinking wine during the Degree Absolute and wonders if the drink was poisoned, by his masters. This is entirely possible: we've seen Number 2s disposed of in the past. McKern's Number 2 spits in Number 1's electronic eye, and tears off his badge. The President consigns him to the smoking dungeon below. He says, 'Be seeing you!' as he descends. Number 2's revolt, the President explains, is 'an established, successful, secure member of the Establishment turning upon and biting the hand that feeds it.' Both types of rebellion are wrong, he insists, and must be eradicated. Now he turns to his third example of rebellion: the former Number 6.

> 'At the other end of the scale, we are honoured to have with us a revolutionary of different calibre. He has Revolted. Resisted. Fought. Held fast. Maintained. Destroyed resistance. Overcome coercion. The right to be a Person, Someone, or Individual, is gloriously epitomised in his person. We applaud his private war and conclude that despite materialistic efforts he has survived, intact and secure. All that remains is recognition of a Man. A Man of steel. A Man magnificently equipped to lead us!'

The President offers The Prisoner a choice: he may leave freely or stay and become Leader of The Village.

On the surveillance screen, we see a 'for sale' sign being removed from the railings outside the house in Buckingham Place. The Prisoner's home is his again. His Lotus is driven up, parked, and polished. In the cave, he is presented with his key, his passport, 'a million' in traveller's cheques (we aren't told whether this is a million pounds or a million dollars – though the pound had recently been 'devalued' it was still worth more than two dollars), and a pouch of petty cash. Up to this moment – ever since he received his suit – The Prisoner has been almost silent, Alice-like, maintaining an ironic smile. Now, urged by the President to make a decision, he doesn't know what to do. Should he stay, or should he go? He can't decide.

Pocketing the bounty, The Prisoner accepts the President's invitation to address the Delegates. He mounts the podium, and starts to speak.

NUMBER 6: 'I feel – '

DELEGATES (in unison): 'Aye! Aye! Aye! Aye!'

He pauses in mid-speech. Waits for the shouting to die down. Begins again. Again the Delegates drown him out with shouts of 'Aye!' – or indeed, 'I', since they are being ordered to be individualists, all at the same time, and in the same way. (As in *Free for All* and *A Change of Mind*, The Prisoner still apparently believes that if one hectors people loudly enough, they will become free-thinking individuals.) Refusing to give up, he delivers an impassioned harangue, entirely drowned out by the non-stop chanting of his fans. I am reminded of The Beatles, who only a year previously had given up touring because the sound of screaming in the big American stadia was so loud and constant, and the PA systems so minimal, that they could not hear their instruments, nor their own voices.

(It *is* possible to hear the first few words of Number 6's speech despite the yelling of the mob. McGoohan begins, 'I feel that, despite the devaluation of the pound, nevertheless...' Economic matters and the value of British currency against the Dollar and the German Mark were currently in the news, but the words feel like placeholders, an improvisation by the actor, not intended to be heard as his final message to the Villagers. Which presumably means his message, whatever it may be, is ultimately irrelevant.)

The Prisoner concludes his speech to the Villagers. No one has heard a word of it. The President bows and invites 'sir' to meet Number 1. Via a rocket-style tube they descend into the tunnels below the giant cave. Down here, guarded by White Helmets, Number 2 and Number 48 quiver in transparent cylinders, labelled Orbit 2 and Orbit 48. Number 48 is singing a fragment of *Dem Bones* while Number 2 laughs repeatedly: unable to see outside their tubes, they are caught in some form of reiterative suspended animation, endlessly replaying their last actions. The President leads The Prisoner up into the capsule atop the rocket. It is full of globes. A masked, robed figure, wearing the 'Number 1' logo we have seen stamped on the fuselage, offers him a fortune teller's crystal ball.

But The Prisoner doesn't want the crystal ball. Instead, he drops it and pulls back the figure's mask and hood – revealing the face of a chimpanzee. But this too is a mask – which The Prisoner pulls away, to reveal his own face. He chases his cackling doppelganger around the capsule. It flees, screeching, into the upper reaches of the ship. Number 6, clearly familiar with the controls of a space rocket, closes the hatch and activates the launch procedure.

Using a fire extinguisher as a weapon, The Prisoner overpowers the guards and frees Number 2 and Number 48 from their mind-control units. With the help of the Butler, they arm themselves with tommy-guns and prepare to exit the rocket and storm the cave. A James Bond-style shootout-in-the-super-villain's-underground-HQ occurs. The battle, with White Helmets running up and falling down, is no worse than the lacklustre battles that end the early Bond movies, and no better. Its ironic intent now clear, *All You Need Is Love* plays on the soundtrack as The Prisoner and his platoon mow the White Helmets down.

Fall Out falls briefly into familiar, action-movie territory – an interesting choice for a series which for the most part studiously avoided this kind of thing. Who are these armed legions, who made their first appearance in *The General*? Has a regime change taken place? First seen guarding a laboratory beneath the Town Hall, the White Helmets are now ubiquitous, riding Mokes with sirens through The Village, operating kidnap squads.

On the streets of The Village, a male voice over the loudspeakers instructs all residents to evacuate. Most of them run for it, on foot. And what of Fenella Fielding? The absence of her dulcet tones suggests that there has been regime change among Number 2's superiors, and that her character is one of the casualties of the coup. Possibly, the cult of Rover, which we saw Village heavies practice in *Arrival*, was viewed as potentially unstable, or subversive. Certainly the stripey-shirted thugs have receded in these final episodes.

Fleets of helicopters rise into the sky – the more important Villagers, departing – and we see our last glimpse of Rover. Once great and terrible, Rover is now a deflating balloon, shrinking back into its primal, bubbling pit, as a comic song repeats the now-official, individualist mantra: 'I – I – I – I – I – I like you very much'. And the rocket is launched.

In the cave, The Prisoner, Number 2 and Number 48 climb into the truck-mounted cage, and the Butler chauffeurs them to freedom – which turns out to be close at hand. Soon they are on the A20, 27 miles from London. They dump their tommy-guns and costumes and dance to the *Dem Bones* song. The Butler pulls over to let Number 48 exit and try to catch a ride. When he has no luck hitching, Number 48 crosses the dual carriageway and thumbs a ride in the opposite direction. His destination is immaterial to him. The Butler drives the truck through Central London. On the banks of the Thames, they are pulled over by a policeman on a moped.

In a long shot, as Number 6 (still doing the *Dem Bones* dance) explains their situation to the constable, Number 2 crosses the road and enters the Houses of Parliament. The Prisoner and the Butler abandon their truck and run to catch a bus back to 1 Buckingham Place. There, the Butler takes up residence, and The Prisoner takes his sports car for a spin.

The last shots of the episode are those which began the series – The Prisoner, at the wheel of his Lotus, racing towards us across an asphalt plain.

WHAT HAVE WE LEARNED?

The word 'fallout' has three meanings: first, it can refer to a set of unintended consequences (as in 'as fallout from the scandal, more resignations occurred'. The escape from The Village fits this concept of fallout); secondly, to 'fall out' is a British military term used to release soldiers on the parade ground from their formation (again, the escape from The Village); thirdly, of course, fallout refers to the radiation scattered widely after the explosion of a nuclear bomb.

All three are possibilities within this episode. The rocket might contain a bomb, though more likely it contains Britain's first astronaut. The Prisoner and his three unlikely allies escape The Village and discover it is on the English coast, a short drive from London. There can be no question as to who ran The Village now. Will there be 'fallout' in the sense of unintended consequences? That is less clear. McKern's Number 2 heads straight for the Houses of Parliament. We see him there twice, first entering the building, then emerging in a bowler hat, pinstripe suit and old-school tie. He is the epitome of the English Establishment: a Whitehall mandarin, or perhaps a member of the House of Lords.

So not only this Number 2, but all the Number 2s, and Fotheringay, and the various Colonels, weren't Russian agents after all, but patriotic Britons, doing their best to break Number 6 on behalf of the burgeoning National Security State. Such men and women will no doubt join the populace in celebrating Britain's first Moon shot. But will The Village's existence ever be revealed? Will the evacuated Villagers tell their stories to *The Listener* and *Daily Mirror*? Or will they simply be picked up, as individuals, and returned to The Village, or to some similar place?

This seems to be McGoohan's conclusion in what can be interpreted as an entirely pessimistic episode. Yes, there has been much excitement and stirring music, and The Village appears to have collapsed, but only after its primary purpose, the rocket launch, has been achieved. The Prisoner has attempted to awaken the Villagers through a spirited address – just as he did in *Free for All* – and they have refused to hear him. Like Ishmael in *Moby Dick*, he has ended up little more than a spectator. He doesn't know whether to leave The Village or remain. When he launches the rocket, is The Prisoner committing the ultimate act of rebellion, or is he doing the job The Village has assigned him? When he and his three friends 'escape', are they, therefore, free? Number 2 returns to his day job, and will continue to display professional interest in people like The Prisoner. Number 48 is destinationless: is he anything beyond what the President called 'uncoordinated youth rebelling against nothing it can define'? Number 6 now has a Butler, and his home has an automatic front door, just like his cottage in The Village. Are these good things?

As the end credits roll, the other principal actors receive single title cards. But McGoohan receives no acting credit. Instead, his card reads, 'Prisoner'. One might call this sour grapes: McGoohan the visionary producer/director/writer has just seen television's most original project – his project

– denied further funding and shut down. In that sense, he is the 'Prisoner' of Lew Grade and of the conservative culture of British television. But I think this extraordinary producer/actor/writer/director chose the title to illustrate his series' conclusion: that Number 6, released from The Village, is still a prisoner. He is a prisoner of London (which will, within a couple of decades, become the self-surveillance capital of the world), a prisoner of Buckingham Place with its Butler and its electric front door, a prisoner of the money he has been given, a prisoner of the traffic which surrounds him, and which will get unbelievably worse, a prisoner of a culture which slavishly celebrates the cult of 'the individual' while rejecting true individuality, a prisoner of an 'entertainment' industry which values repetition and familiarity above originality and genius.

Be seeing you...

DECODING *THE PRISONER*

It would be fair to say that nobody 'got' *The Prisoner* when it first aired on British TV. We watched the episodes in black-and-white, in the wrong order. A series of such mystery and complexity demands multiple viewings (something broadcast television didn't offer in those days) and considerable thought. It was said that the last episode infuriated British viewers and that TV station switchboards were 'jammed with complaints'. I don't know if that was really true. I was thrilled by the life and energy and originality of *Fall Out*, even if I didn't know what it all meant. Quite possibly, the enraged viewers were another myth, to justify the abrupt ending of the only TV series that ever mattered. The Americans had it worse, even though they saw *The Prisoner* in colour. The episodes were further reshuffled, and *Living in Harmony* wasn't screened.

Today it's possible to watch the episodes in an order which begins to make sense of them. With the exception of *Once Upon A Time*, this is the order in which they were filmed. And it's possible, then, to suggest a meaning to those episodes, and to the series as a whole. So here goes...

George Markstein, in his script 'bible', wrote: 'Our hero is a man who held a highly confidential job of the most secret nature. He therefore has knowledge which is invaluable or highly dangerous, depending on which side he falls.' What was that job?

The Prisoner is a rocket scientist. His highly-confidential job was working for the British government on a British rocket project. Like many people involved in rocketry – including Wernher von Braun, who worked first for the Nazis, employing slave labour in a concentration camp, and then for the Americans – he is an enthusiastic proponent of space travel, and once hoped that he would be selected as an astronaut aboard a British Moon mission. But there is a dark side to rocket science: it is 'dual use' technology, and the same giant, multi-stage rockets which can send men to the Moon are also the delivery systems of thermonuclear bombs. Von Braun had no problem with this. His primary interest may have been space travel, but he was also an ardent proponent of nuclear weapons, and proposed numerous methods of destroying Russia, including orbiting atom bomb platforms in space. As Tom Lehrer put it,

> 'I just send them up,
> Who knows where they come down?
> That's not my department,
> Says Wernher von Braun.'

The Prisoner is a man considerably more moral and courageous than the despicable von Braun. Having aspired to be an astronaut, and having put his considerable engineering skills to work on the secret British rocket project – which like von Braun's missiles can be used for space travel or for species extinction – Number 6 had second thoughts. 'Too many people' know about the supposed secret: the leaky British Establishment had increased the danger of proliferation, and thus the likelihood of nuclear war.

So he resigned.

Who runs The Village? The Brits, of course. Number 6 knows too much, and British 'intelligence' has extrajudicially rendered him to a 'black site' similar to the one Markstein heard of – with a couple of differences. The Village is within a few hours' drive from London, and it is not a home for superannuated spies, but a prison for scientists – a high-technology park where they can be forced to continue their researches, and to reveal what secrets they may have spilled. In its enclosed environment, high-tech drones and surveillance systems are developed; mind control methods are perfected; and potentially profitable spin-offs such as Speedlearn are beta-tested on the imprisoned populace. The most critical of all these high-tech projects is the British rocket, which is being built in one of the deep bunkers beneath The Village. Though The Prisoner doesn't know it, his rocket project has been designated 'Number 1'.

Who is Number 1? The rocket is Number 1! Only twice in the series is Number 1 referred to as a person – once the Colonel in Dr. Seltzman's body, and once in *Fall Out*, in an exchange between Number 6 and McKern's Number 2:

NUMBER 6: 'Did you ever meet him? Did you ever meet Number 1?'

NUMBER 2: 'Face to face?'

NUMBER 6: 'Yes.'

NUMBER 2: 'Meet "him"?' (laughs)

At which point, the rocket summons his attention with a green light and a siren.

Number 2 asks Number 6, 'Shall I give him a stare?' He is speaking of the rocket, and – in his defiance – he spits in its blinking, robot eye. In McGoohan's words, 'it boasts a modest appellation, being the figure 1 (one) writ large on its side,' so I assume that this is British Lunar Mission Number 1: the ship The Prisoner once hoped to pilot, a race directly to the Moon, beating the Americans and the Russians there. Moon missions were on his mind in *The Chimes of Big Ben* and in *Do Not Forsake Me* too. And Number 1 is designed for space travel: nuclear missiles don't have pilots' capsules or men in monkey suits on board.

Who is the man in the monkey suit? McGoohan's script describes the individual as having 'his own face. Bestial in expression.' He describes their struggle as 'seemingly a fight between man and a beast.' When they meet, in a two-shot, the hooded figure is a head shorter than The Prisoner. We know that The Village authorities are able to clone humans or make copies of them. This was done to The Prisoner himself in *The Schizoid Man*. Extrapolating from this, I would suggest that after he quit his job working for the government as a rocket scientist, some ironist within the apparat decided to give the 'Lunarnaut' The Prisoner's facial characteristics. It was common practice in those early space missions to send dogs or apes into orbit: sometimes provision was even made for their return to Earth. I believe that the 'astronaut' whom Number 6 chases around the space capsule may be an intelligent ape, given his facial appearance by the diabolical doctors in The Village Hospital. Why does the ape/astronaut have the '1' logo on his robe? Because he is part of British Lunar Mission Number 1. Colonels Armstrong, Aldrin and Collins all wore patches reading 'Apollo 11'. This did not mean *they* were Apollo 11. It was their mission's name.

What is the significance of the Penny Farthing bicycle, logo of The Village? In the 1960s, this antique bicycle was still thought of as a British invention: in fact, it was invented by a Frenchman. Either way it serves, obviously, as an example of 'old tech'. If The Village is a technology park filled with rendered scientists, the Penny Farthing represents a starting point for their labours: early British technology, rooted in a charming, quasi-rural and imaginary past, in which our scientist-prisoners must flourish, and do their best work. This was the honest goal of the British soap magnate, Henry Lever, when he ordered the construction of a fantastically picturesque workers' village, 'Port Sunlight', to contain his workforce in attractive, company-owned homes of diverse styles, adjacent to the factory. Port Sunlight, on the Wirral Peninsula, is quite lovely and worth a visit, just like Portmeirion.

And what of 'Pop'? The word appears in the title of a nursery rhyme, played more than once during the series, and is spoken repeatedly during Number 2's attempt to crack Number 6 using the Degree Absolute process. Number 2 suggests it means 'Protect Other People'. But there is an additional use of the word in *The Prisoner*, known only to those ardent *aficionados* who have watched the early cuts of *Arrival* and *Chimes of Big Ben*. The closing credits of the broadcast series end with a shot of Rover bubbling up, then coasting across the sea. These were late, ungraceful additions. Originally the credits ended with a pull-out revealing a kitsch view of the Solar System, featuring multiple ringed planets. Then Planet Earth fills the frame, the word 'Pop' is superimposed, and the credits end. The original images can still be enjoyed in those two 'first cuts'. What do they mean? The pull-out to the Solar System reinforces the notion of a space mission, I believe. White and Ali, in *The Official Prisoner Companion*, suggest that this was McGoohan's apocalyptic vision, and that at the end of the credits the universe explodes. In fact, when one views the alternate credits, the universe doesn't explode. The word 'Pop' is superimposed over Earth alone. Nevertheless, I think White and Ali are basically right: 'Pop' is indeed a warning that our most prized technology may destroy us – that the same technology which sends a man-ape to the Moon can rain a firestorm of nuclear missiles upon the Earth.

Why was the 'Pop' ending deleted, in favour of two out-takes of Rover? Because it tells us too much about the meaning of *The Prisoner*? Because it was apocalyptic, and ITC requested its removal? Or because, after *Arrival* and *Chimes* were screened for journalists prior to the series' broadcast, they focused too much on the 'Pop' and not enough on the episodes themselves?

It's been suggested that *The Prisoner* is a religious prophecy. It is said that McGoohan was a Christian, and the last words of his script for *Fall Out* are those of the Spiritual song *Dem Bones*: 'Now hear the word of the Lord.' I find this unconvincing, having grown up in England, which is officially a Christian country, and where Christian instruction was compulsory in state schools. In reality, Christianity is often just the icing on the cake of conquest, but in theory it is a religion of love: its prophet, Jesus, said repeatedly that love was all one needed. There is no love to speak of in *The Prisoner*. The Prisoner loves no one (except in the contradictory episode *Do Not Forsake Me*, in which McGoohan barely appears). 'Love' in *Checkmate* is a false emotion with which the Queen is programmed – a product of Village mind control. Mme. Professor's 'love' for her husband in *The General* is meaningless: she does nothing to save him from being worked to death.

McGoohan's use of The Beatles' song *All You Need Is Love* is chilling: first as a cacophonous 'ditty', then as background music as the White Helmets are tommy-gunned. For The Beatles, the song was sincere in its intention, as a riposte to the violence of the Vietnam War, and its domestic fallout. McGoohan subverts the song – and why not? But what results is not a message of love. *Dem Bones* the song refers to a passage of Ezekiel, a book of the Old Testament. If this is religious prophecy, it is Old Testament prophecy, of a violent and apocalyptic kind. The series *The Prisoner* doesn't feel, to me, like any kind of religious prophecy. It reads like a prophetic critique of *secular* society and science, and the direction in which they were/are headed.

The Village can be viewed in an alternative mystical light: not a place of Prophecy, but one dedicated to Ritual. This is a society which has taken science as its religion, and its top secret science project – British Lunar Mission Number 1 – is also its deepest religious mystery. There is a myriad of ritualistic aspects attendant to Number 6's imprisonment in The Village. The opening sequence – viewed repeatedly by us, as we absorb the episodes – takes on a ritualistic quality, preparing us for the next *Prisoner* adventure and allowing us our first glimpse of the New Number 2. There are rituals of language – from 'I am a free man' and 'Be seeing you!' to exchanges of meaningless numbers and words – and of activity, as Social Progress Clubs, art therapy groups, Speedlearn devotees, and the occasional mob all demonstrate. The Village has darker rituals, too, more reminiscent of the Aztecs and the Borgias: it tortures people to death, or brain-death; it disappears people; it tries different mind control techniques on a captive population. The Prisoner – who fights to retain his Village number, and never once speaks his own name – becomes the hero of the Ritual of The Village. His indecision, in *Fall Out*, is like that of Orpheus in Cocteau's film. There, *Orphée* falls in love with Death, and wants to remain with her, in Hades. Given the chance of freedom, Number 6 half-desires to remain within The Village, on this comfortable throne, enjoying the secrets of the Cave.

In such a reading, when he accepts the invitation to address the Delegates, when he climbs aboard the 'Number 1', and when he launches the rocket, The Prisoner is playing the part that has been expected of him all along. He has taken the hero's journey, from Recent Recruit to Maximum Villager. Number 6: launcher of Lunar expeditions, liberator of prisoners.

Or is our nameless protagonist still the defiant individualist, sabotaging the mission by launching the rocket too soon, against its masters' wishes, provoking the panicked liberation of the Villagers, most of whom would rather stay, and the destruction of their prison? Unmutual Number 6!

Who is Number 6?

EPILOGUE

I see *The Prisoner* now as a kind of shark tank. Within it, gigantic talents circled each other. The foremost was McGoohan, who revealed himself as perhaps the most brilliant and original writer/director ever to work in British television. But other serious talents circled that tank, too: many fine actors, including McKern, Muscat, and Stock; Markstein, the story editor; Tobias-Shaw, the casting director; Shampan, the production designer.

Outside that shark tank was another, larger tank: the dramatic world of London in the late 1960s – the most exciting period of British drama since the Jacobeans. In that tank circled Lindsay Anderson (whose films *If....* and *O Lucky Man!* were clearly influenced by *The Prisoner*), Ken Loach and other talented BBC directors, Ken Russell with his documentaries and upcoming espionage feature, *Billion Dollar Brain*; Nicolas Roeg (who would shortly shoot and co-direct *Performance*, another British feature hard to imagine without *The Prisoner*); Peter Watkins (director of the magnificent *War Game*, already blackballed by the BBC); Tony Richardson, whose *Loneliness of the Long Distance Runner* was a work of genius of a very different kind; the writers Harold Pinter and Samuel Beckett; Orson Welles, who had directed West End theatre, and who never missed an opportunity to wine and dine in London; Lew Grade, the independent TV impresario, who threw his massive fiscal energy behind McGoohan and *The Prisoner*. They knew each other and each other's work, in some cases intimately. They watched each other like hawks, and circled their London tank, shark-like.

Beyond that tank, in darkness, swam flatter, fatter fishes, who knew nothing: the British and American TV gatekeepers, who hated originality and genuine talent, whose only ability was the negative one of denying money, of shutting things down.

In 1966 and 1967, *The Prisoner* was the most interesting game in town. *2001* was being shot at MGM at the same time, but it was an American show with an American director. There was no entrée there for London-based writing or directing talents. *The Prisoner* was different: home-grown, episodic drama with multiple positions for directors and writers. What if McGoohan had opened the doors of his shark tank to let some of those other sharks swim in? What if he had invited Watkins or Richardson – visionary brother directors – to direct an episode? What if he had taken more interest in the scripts and asked Pinter, or Beckett, whom he clearly admired, to write *Once Upon A Time*? What if he had asked Nic Roeg to shoot *Fall Out*? What if he had invited the peripatetic Welles to direct *The Schizoid Man*?

Working with such talents would not have been without its problems. Quite possibly some of the above-named would have declined the invitation. But any one of them would have brought their individual genius to *The Prisoner*, and made a great series greater still. One of the ironies of *The Prisoner* is that McGoohan, an individual making a show about individuals, was content to hire some second-rate, seriously un-individualistic talents. A greater irony is that, with the fate of the series still uncertain, its creator may have lost direction, or interest, and tried to find validation by leaping out of the tank. McGoohan left *The Prisoner* in hands less able than his own, to act in a big-budget Hollywood film which nobody remembers. Lew Grade offered Everyman Films £900,000 to develop and produce two theatrical features: Ibsen's *Brand*, starring McGoohan, and a thriller set in Ireland. Neither film was made. McGoohan moved to Los Angeles and acted in a dozen films and some TV shows, turning in more two-speed performances. He did not change or develop as an actor. He did not become a movie star. He directed a feature version of *Othello: Catch My Soul*. He made some money. And so what? As Mr Bernstein says in *Citizen Kane*, it's not hard to make a million dollars, if that's the only thing you care about.

And what of us, the viewers? Where do we fit into this – as anything beyond passive consumers of an entertainment celebrating individualism? When I first watched *The Prisoner* I was stunned and inspired. Over those seventeen weeks I learned that TV could be more – a lot more – than the repetitive, generic rubbish I had been largely fed up to that point. I wanted to jump into that shark tank. As soon as I could, I did. I have yet to emerge. I became a prisoner of *The Prisoner*, like many others who saw it and were fascinated, and who were, in some weird way, transformed by it.

In conclusion, I'll try and address the feeling of desperate sadness which seems to surround The Prisoner's escape in the last episode. I felt this sadness when I watched *Fall Out* at the ripe old age of 13, and again yesterday, re-watching it at 62 years young. *Fall Out* is replete with references to the Summer of Love – how much did Lew Grade have to pay to license *All You Need Is Love*? McGoohan knew that something was going on, and liked Alexis Kanner, whose character seems to represent, for him, the Hippie spirit. Trying to hitch a ride along the dual carriageway, it's clear Number 48 doesn't care which way he travels as long as he's going *somewhere*. Yet no one stops to offer him a ride. And, at the end of the show, there's no love, no revolution, no change, only continuance.

The Prisoner regains the racing car he built for himself, and his London town house. The faithful Butler takes up residence there. McKern's Number 2 returns to Parliament. So much has happened, and yet, in that very English way, nothing has changed at all.

As Number 6 and Dutton observed in *Dance of the Dead*:

DUTTON: 'How's London?'

NUMBER 6: 'About the same.'

DUTTON: 'Yeah… places don't change. Only people.'

Yet everything changed. Anyone who visits Parliament today, with its bomb-proof crash barriers, surveillance cameras, security guards and armed police, can see where the Imperial Project has led us over the last fifty years. A few years back I and a small crew were stopped and cautioned by the London police for pointing a video camera at the Houses of Parliament from across the Thames. In 1967, McGoohan, McKern and company just showed up, without permission, and shot *The Prisoner*'s closing sequence there. The scene had been scheduled well in advance, but the crew decided simply to 'wing it' on a Sunday morning. The story goes that they even inveigled a puzzled police constable to be a supporting actor in the scene.

A few days later, the production received a stern letter from Parliament's Serjeant-at-Arms, accusing them of shooting without a permit. An assistant director was sent to apologise. Fortunately the two men had both been in the British Navy. They had a jolly time exchanging reminiscences, *The Prisoner* was granted a retroactive shooting permit, and all was well. As previously observed, Britain in the 1960s and 1970s suffered from occasional acts of terrorism: the IRA set off bombs, and people were sometimes killed. But we did not live in terror of terror in those days.

The scene outside Parliament has the look of the times – it's Sunday 19 November, 1967, and the morning air seems either polluted or foggy, probably both. And yet the city is also calm, and uncrowded, and untrafficked. *The Prisoner* was made when one could still, apparently, knock on Londoners' doors and ask to speak to the 'master' or the 'mistress' of the house. And the Mother of Parliaments was protected by a lone, young copper who could be persuaded to act as an extra in your film.

Freedom of movement, freedom to point a camera, freedom from detention without charge, freedom to enter a building without being pushed, filed, indexed, stamped, briefed, debriefed and numbered by uniformed security sentinels, all this and much more has been swept away. What is London today but The Village, surveilled, monitored, under the watchful eyes of private security companies, the police, MI5, GCHQ, NSA, and all the other acronyms which give us limited permission to function according to their terms? *HM Open Prison London*

- *ID Mandatory At All Times.* Who is Number 1? Who benefits? McGoohan, the British outsider, gave us a chilling vision of what might be in store for us, if we failed to act as thoughtful individuals: a culture of mass entertainment silliness, focused on fashion, exploited for great gain, where sedated politicians stumble through meaningless elections, and journalists fake the news. Somehow, from this sorry and manipulated vision of the near future, he made a TV entertainment which puzzled and inspired more than one generation, and which has lost none of its verve, wit, prescience, and melancholy in the intervening fifty years.

ACKNOWLEDGEMENTS

The author is forever in the debt of Ion Mills and Claire Watts for their extraordinary support and guidance, and to Elsa Mathern for her expert design and typesetting skills.

For further information about the series, the reader may visit The Unmutual and Six of One sites.

theunmutual.co.uk
sixofone.co.uk

INDEX

ABOUT US

In addition to Kamera Books, Oldcastle Books has a number of other imprints, including No Exit Press, Creative Essentials, Pulp! The Classics, Pocket Essentials and High Stakes Publishing **> oldcastlebooks.co.uk**

Checkout the kamera film salon for independent, arthouse and world cinema **> kamera.co.uk**

For more information, media enquiries and review copies please contact Clare **> marketing@oldcastlebooks.com**